The Use of Strategic Planning
for Churches and Ministries

by
R. Henry Migliore
Facet Enterprises Professor of
Strategic Planning and Management
Northeastern State University/University Center at Tulsa

Tulsa, Oklahoma

The Use of Strategic Planning for Churches and Ministries
ISBN 0-89274-513-4
Copyright © 1988 by
R. Henry Migliore
Managing for Success
P. O. Box 957
Jenks, Oklahoma 74037

Published by Harrison House
P. O. Box 35035
Tulsa, Oklahoma 74153

Contents

Foreword

The future is ours to see — although we are tempted to say, "Only God knows the future."

But we *can* see the future through a glass darkly. By planning and dreaming, we of the Church need not be like crabs on the beach, looking only where we have been and backing into the future.

The office and function of the prophet can be fulfilled as we "think God's thoughts after Him" individually and collectively.

Dr. Migliore's, *The Use of Strategic Planning in Churches and Ministries* can save your church from saying to its prophet, "You go into the presence of God that He may speak to you, but let not God speak to us lest we die!"

The concepts in this book can surface more plans for the future in you and your staff than you knew were there. What is more, they will be your plans anointed by God.

Because the Holy Spirit began to be "poured out upon all flesh" at Pentecost, your church or ministry can unite its leaders in hearing from God for its unique future. Old Testament theocracy can be replaced by New Testament consensus.

The God that brought Israel out of Egypt indwells us to lead us on. Through prayer and this unique

planning you will discover He is not the God above —
He is the God ahead.

James B. Buskirk, S.T.D.
Pastor and Senior Minister
The First United Methodist Church
Tulsa, Oklahoma

Preface

During the winter of 1977-78 a new dimension was added to my own ministry of helping organizations and individuals with management and planning. I had just completed a seminar in Tulsa, Oklahoma, on *Strategic Planning* and *Management by Objectives*. The late Dr. L. D. Thomas, Jr., was in the audience. I had known him and had heard him preach at Tulsa's First United Methodist Church.

He said, "We need this (Strategic Planning and Management by Objectives) at First Methodist."

At a meeting later, we discussed the aspects of these seminars as they might affect churches. I felt confident with railroads, coal mines, manufacturers, oil companies, and so forth, but I did not feel that I had the experience or background to assist a church. However, Dr. Thomas persuaded me to help, and I accepted with a sense of anticipation and excitement.

Jan Ausdemore, a student at the time and now owner of his own business, joined the First Methodist staff to help coordinate and implement the planning process called "Ministry by Objectives." Since that time a large number of my students have assisted churches and ministries with planning under my direction.

From this beginning I have had the opportunity to work with several major ministries and hundreds of smaller ministries and churches. During 1987, I assisted major planning and objective setting efforts at Victory Christian Center, Tulsa, Oklahoma; Mother

Tucker's House of Prayer, Tulsa; and Calvary Temple, Tampa, Florida. I also assisted the First United Methodist Church, Tulsa, and First Presbyterian Church, Tulsa. Jeff Horvath and Lisa Mitchell, recent MBA graduates, played a major role in each project.

My assistance with these organizations has been in the area of professional management. I have left the theological questions for more informed minds. My prayer is that these concepts will help Christians in planning and organizing their work so they can attain their greatest potential for serving the Lord.

R. Henry Migliore
Jenks, Oklahoma
February 1988

Abstract

Strategic Planning and *Management by Objectives* (MBO) have been many things to many different people. The two concepts have been combined and have evolved from contributions made by practitioners, scholars, and businessmen. The notion that strategic planning provides a broader scale for the usual concept of MBO is described. This book discusses how this philosophy of management can be used in church and ministry administration. Actual experiences of a number of churches and ministries are described.

This book is designed to help ministry leaders and their churches or organizations achieve their potential and meet the needs of the people involved by:

— Getting a plan in writing

— Getting people involved and committed to the plan

— Freeing the time of senior and associate pastors or ministry heads to do what they have been called to do

— Creating an organization that is productive and efficient

— Meeting the needs of the regular pastors and staff.

Biblical Backup to Planning and Management

Commit your work to the Lord, then it will succeed.

Any enterprise is built by wise planning.

Proverbs 16:3; 24:3 TLB

May he grant you your heart's desire and fulfill all your plans.

Psalm 20:4 TLB

The Lord Almighty has sworn,

Surely, as I have planned, so it will be, and as I have purposed, so it will stand.

Isaiah 14:24,25 NIV

. . . What I have planned, that will I do. . . .

Isaiah 46:11

Where there is no vision, the people perish: but he that keepeth the law, happy is he.

Proverbs 29:18

. . . And your young men shall see visions, and your old men shall dream dreams.

Acts 2:17

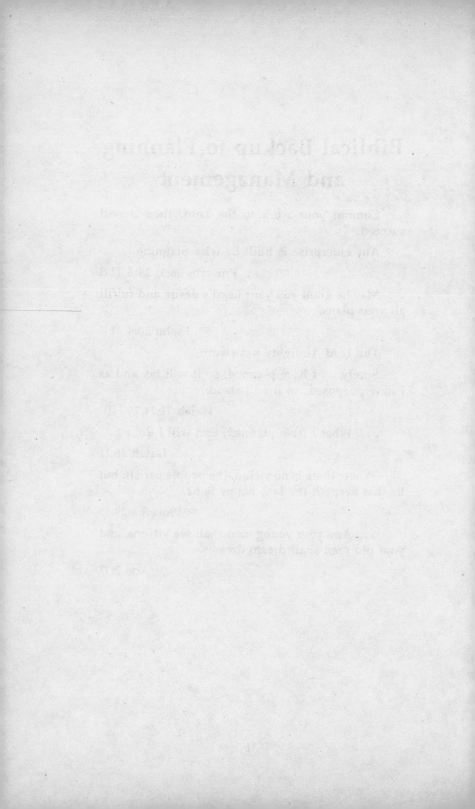

Biblical Back-up to: Planning and Management

Commit your work to the Lord, then it will
succeed.

Any enterprise is built by wise planning...

Proverbs 16:3, 24:3 TLB

May he shall you your heart's desire and fulfill
all your plans.

Psalm 20:4

The Lord Almighty has sworn,

Surely, as I have planned, so it will be, and as
I have proposed, so it will stand.

Isaiah 14:24

What I have decided, that I will do...

Isaiah 46:11

...this is in the last days, the sensible person that
builds their house upon a rock, longer to be...

Matthew 7:24-25

...but your young men shall see visions, and
your old men shall dream dreams.

Acts 2:17

Introduction:
Laying Out a Straight Flight Path

If you are struggling with any of the following problems or have these questions, this book, *The Use of Strategic Planning in Churches and Ministries*, may be very important to you.

Why is there so much confusion among the associate pastors on what we are trying to accomplish?

Why is there so much dissension and disagreement in the church?

Why is there such a turnover of people in the church, especially in leadership positions?

Why did we build that building when it is not being used?

As a pastor, why am I working twelve hours a day and can never keep up?

Why have we failed on a number of projects and missions?

Why did God let us down?

Why is the devil stopping us?

Why have the elders asked me to resign after everything I have put into this church or ministry?

Why does this church lack enthusiasm?

If you are struggling with one of these questions, the answer might be the lack of good long-term strategic planning. Part of strategic planning is the team-building approach of developing leaders and having the people involved in the plan. I especially like the approach Jim Durkin takes in the chapter, "Building With Long-Term Plans" from the book, *The Master Builder* (9, p. 45). He says:

When I took up flying an airplane years ago, I did not have the advantage of the radios and instruments that are common in small planes today. Pilots of small planes had to fly by visual flight rules. This meant that after take-off, the plane had to be oriented in the right direction by some visual landmark. While the compass could point the general direction, it was not reliable.

Simply following the compass would cause the plane to swerve back and forth in a wide, zig-zag pattern. Being magnetic, the compass needle would tend to sway. It couldn't provide steady direction because of its short-term gyrations. If a pilot tried to follow it strictly, he might never reach his destination, especially if fuel was limited.

To keep on a straight and steady flight path, I was taught how to pick out a visual landmark, perhaps a mountain or some other feature that could be seen fifty miles out on the horizon. By keeping my eyes fixed on that landmark, I could keep the plane steady and moving straight toward a long-range destination.

I use this analogy because it so clearly illustrates the effect of either a short- or long-term perspective; one is choppy, erratic and wastes fuel; the other guides the plane on a steady, constant and certain course.

A church without a long-term perspective will follow the same pattern. Instead of moving with steadiness and certainty toward God's goals, it will continually swerve off course. It will be caught up with every wind of doctrine that blows through — the latest teaching fad, the newest conspiracy theory, a new teaching on Communism, new studies on the anti-Christ, new faith teachings. There is an endless supply of distractions that will take a church off the course of pursuing God's purpose and vision. Just as one new fad passes, another springs up.

Success Depends on the Vision, Perspective, and Plan

Durkin sums up the philosophy and direction of this book. For everyone to be successful — the elders, the pastor, the congregation — a vision, long-term perspective, and a plan are desperately needed for success. If you look at the mistakes of the past, it is obvious that many churches and ministries have followed this zig-zag pattern Durkin speaks of. In ten years of consulting with churches and ministries, I have observed this exact pattern in a large number of organizations. If you take the time and effort to read this book, follow up on your people, apply the format prescribed here, and prayerfully keep God in every step of the plan, here is what I believe you can expect:

1. A sense of enthusiasm in your church or ministry

2. A five-year plan in writing to which everyone is committed

3. A sense of commitment by the entire church to its overall direction

4. Job duties and responsibilities will be clear

5. Time for the leaders to do what they have been called to do

6. Clear and evident improvement in the health and vitality of every member of the management team

7. Measurable improvement in the personal lives of all those in responsible positions with time for vacations, family, and personal pursuits

8. The ability to measure very specifically the growth and contribution made by senior pastors or evangelists at the close of their careers

9. Guaranteed leadership of the church or ministry, because a plan is in place in writing and is understood — even more importantly, a management team will be in place to guide the church or ministry into its next era of growth.

It is important to understand the origin of — and something about — *Management By Objectives* and *Strategic Long-Range Planning* (SLRP). Both concepts are combined and adapted for church and ministry use. Many Christians who work for major corporations that use these concepts will recognize the principles in this book. There is help in every congregation. Pastors and church leaders can receive valuable assistance from members experienced in the use of these concepts.

MBO was first used as an acronym in 1954 by Peter Drucker (8). However, many elements used in MBO were actually developed earlier. Various authors, managers, and consultants contributed to the growth and acceptance of MBO. George Odiorne, Dale D. McConkey, George Morrisey, and others are credited with giving MBO a substantial boost circa 1965. Odiorne defined management by objectives as "a process whereby the superior and subordinate managers of an organization jointly identify its (the organization's) common goals, define each person's major area of responsibility in terms of the results expected of him, and use these measures as guides for operating the unit and assessing the contribution of each of its members" (38, p.55).

An even broader definition would consider the firm's purpose, the environment in which it operates, and its strengths and weaknesses. Moreover, assumptions would be made before setting objectives.

Based on these definitions, the following specific elements in MBO can be identified: planning, objectives and goals, negotiation, performance review, and evaluation.

I propose a new definition of the term: "MBO is a philosophy of management based on identifying purpose, objectives, and desired results; establishing a realistic program for obtaining these results; and evaluating performance in achieving them." The version described in this book will be called "Strategic Long-Range Planning/MBO" (SLRP/MBO).

The following nine-point breakdown of this SLRP/MBO definition is the most complete to appear in one place, and by its inclusion of a specific preobjective-setting process, it makes MBO at all levels a more grounded and realistic system capable of creating true change in attitudes as well as in productivity. The definition is adapted for ministry use.

Such a philosophy involves:

1. Defining a ministry purpose and reason for being

2. Monitoring the environment in which it operates

3. Realistically assessing its strengths and weaknesses

4. Making assumptions about unpredictable future events

5. Prescribing written, specific, and measurable objectives in principal result areas contributing to the organization's purpose

a. Negotiating and bargaining at every level of leadership and staff position

b. Recognizing a performance contract embracing the agreed-upon objectives

6. Developing strategies on how to use available resources to meet objectives

7. Making long- and short-range plans to meet objectives

a. Normal budgeting process in this stage

b. PERT, Project Management, old time MBO

8. Constantly appraising performance to determine whether it is keeping pace with attainment of objectives and is consistent with defined purpose

a. Willingness to change or modify objectives, strategies, and plans when conditions change

b. Evaluating progress at every stage so that needed changes can be made smoothly

c. Making sure that rewards are thoughtfully considered and are appropriate for the accomplishment, and recognizing the strengths and weaknesses of the extrinsic and intrinsic rewards

9. Reevaluating purpose, environment, strengths, weaknesses, and assumptions before setting objectives for the next performance year.

Figure 1.1 shows how the process interacts. This figure is adapted from *An MBO Approach to Long-Range Planning and Long-Range Strategic Planning*. (Note pp. 70,72.)

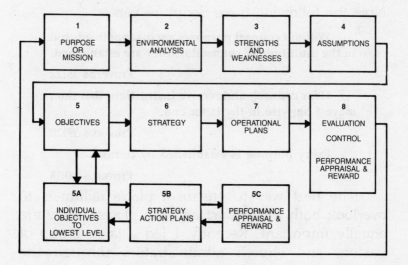

The following discussion will cover each of these nine points in detail: (1) its importance, (2) the mechanics of using it, and finally, (3) examples to help the church pastor and administrator grasp each concept.

A True Vision Must Be Shared

It is important to recognize at this point what I call "the two Ps." The "Ps" represent *Product and Process.* *Product* means "get the plan in writing." The plan must be something you can hold in your hand, a written product of your efforts. If the plan is not in writing, I call it daydreaming. When it is in writing, you are telling yourself and others you are serious about it. The second "P" represents *Process:* every plan must have maximum input from everyone. Those who execute the plan must be *in* the plan. The Bible tells us to get input. Note the following three Scripture verses:

Without counsel purposes are disappointed: but in the multitude of counsellors they are established.

Proverbs 15:22

Hear counsel, and receive instruction, that thou mayest be wise in thy latter end.

Proverbs 19:20

Every purpose is established by counsel.

Proverbs 20:18

The best way to ensure a plan's failure is to overlook both the *product* and the *process.* They are equally important. Recently, I led a large group of pastors and church administrators through the planning process outlined in this article. The response was positive and reflected the need for improved planning and management in ministries. (Note their comments in Appendix A.) In a survey of 286 Charismatic nondenominational pastors in 1985, 98.5 percent felt that strategic long-range planning and objective setting were important. However, the survey reported that only 43 percent had objectives with 28 percent in writing, 49 percent had a budget, with 36 percent having short-range planning meetings. A total of 9 percent had planning meetings that focused on three to five years.

The Greatest Needs of Today's Ministries and Churches

In surveying a group of twenty-three pastors from a denominational church in 1986, 96 percent felt that long-range planning and objective setting were important. Other results revealed the following: 77 percent set objectives, and of these, 88 percent put them in writing. All of those surveyed had a budget, with 74 percent having held short-range planning meetings. A total of 26 percent had planning meetings that focused on three to five years. In a 1987 study of denominational churches, we found 37.8 percent felt they had a long-range plan and 81.1 percent had a short-range plan. All had a yearly budget.

Both denominational and non-denominational pastors appeared to be unanimous in their beliefs that strategic long-range planning is important. To put matters into perspective, let us try to translate church-and-ministry success into a formula. In this case X is success, a dependent variable, and is on the left side of the equation. The = sign means a balance, or equal to what is on the other side; the F means "a function of." On the right side are all the independent variables:

A. Pastor as Spiritual Leader

B. Pastor as Manager

C. Planning System

D. Control System

E. Location

F. Needs of People Met

G. Denomination's National Influence

H. Denomination's Local Influence

I. Obedience, courage (Joshua 1:8).

Expressing this in the form of a formula:

$$X = F (A, B, C, D, E, F, H, I - \text{on to Infinity}).$$

X, or "the dependent variable," can be described as success for the church. Of course, it is beyond the scope of this discussion to define success. The variables *A* through *Infinity*, which we can identify, are the "independent variables."

Only a few variables are listed, but the possibilities are endless. Also, I am assuming here that success is not necessarily equated to size. I am making the definition of success broader than church members, budget, and so forth. There seems to be a widespread notion that size is the only barometer, but I do not hold to that belief.

God has raised up many spiritual leaders. I believe the greatest problems holding back these leaders — and the churches and ministries they serve — involve some combination of independent variables *B, C, and D.* Planning, management, organization, and control are some of the greatest needs of churches and ministries today.

I am assuming that every pastor is to some degree a spiritual leader, or he could not remain in the pulpit. However, his entire ministry and the success of his church are then in direct proportion to variables B, C, *and D.* If you assume all other variables are constant and full effort goes into B, C, *and D,* then the X factor (success), the dependent variable, has to go up. Without training and knowledge in the area of planning and management, the church and ministry have a ceiling on success. No organization can get any bigger than the capacity of its managers to manage. The hindrance is not the needs of the people — because they are always there. It is not the denomination or location, it is plainly planning, management, organization, and control.

If every pastor and evangelist could learn and improve each of these areas just a little each year, they could be much more successful. They could reduce drastically all the obvious errors in direction, false starts, wasted efforts, frustrated staff members, and waste. J. Peter Grace, chairman and president of W. R. Grace Corp. and head of the President's Commission on Waste in Government, would have a field day if he took his team into the religious world looking for waste and inefficiency.

I hear a lot of Christians these days saying, "The devil is holding us back."

Sorry, I think the devil sleeps late and rests while we run around in circles. He does not need to work hard.

To give due credit, Bill Lowrey, the founder and director of *Christ Is The Answer,* headquartered in El Paso, Texas, shared with me the results achieved by one

23

of his teams in Mexico. The team was holding services daily and doing its work at a cost of $29 per person per month. This is inspiring to see what can be done with so little.

I do not think Christians should wait until someone comes along and creates a big scandal about waste and inefficiency. We need to put our shoulders to the wheel and pay attention to planning, management, organization, control, and people. If we do not, on the whole, the church will accomplish in the next fifty years about what it did in the last fifty years — maintain the status quo.

My observation is that many people in ministry and church work are reluctant to plan, do not want a plan in writing, and do not ask for advice. The tendency is to be led by "the Spirit" which is sometimes a whim or emotional impulse. This reflects our general American inclination to "hang loose." Some 75 percent of the profit-making organizations I have worked with have the same problem. The 25 percent that have the discipline to plan and manage properly, far out perform those that do not. Higher profits, better service, fewer turnovers are but a few of the rewards. I think the same good fortune comes to those ministries and churches that have the discipline to plan and manage properly.

Many times I hear "the devil is fighting us" when a plan or project goes sour. I am not discounting a demon force, but in many instances the devil does not need to fight Christians. We are our own worst enemies. Many failures can be traced to poor planning, lack of getting people involved in the planning, and generally, poor management. I often sense a spirit of extreme urgency in church ministry planning. This is used as a "go for it — if it is of the Lord, it will prosper" mentality. What is the rush? Many churches and ministries need to slow down, plan, and pray. Often they have rushed around in circles for the past few years. I do not believe God will give His best until we give our best. Included in doing our best is using the best planning and management philosophies and techniques available.

Why should a church or ministry devote time to planning? Questions I ask are:

"Do you know where you are going and how you are going to get there?"

"Does everyone know what you are trying to accomplish?"

"Does everyone know what is expected of them?"

If the answer to any of these is no, then you need to develop a strategic long-range plan with as many people involved as possible. I agree with Alvin J. Lingren who observed in his book entitled *Foundations for Purposeful Church Administration*:

> It is easily observed that most churches do not engage in such systematic long-range planning. Perhaps this is one reason why the church has not been able to reach and change society more effectively. Many churches operate on hand-to-mouth planning. They consider the pressing problems of the moment at each board meeting without placing them in proper perspective in relationship to either past or future. (23, p. 226)

Long-Range Planning Can Be a Means of Renewal

He then goes on to say that "long-range planning, then, becomes a means of renewal in the life of a congregation" (23, p. 231). Also included in this book is the importance of dreams and visions for a church, as well as studies of the environment, involvement from the congregation, and implementation of the plan. These points are in agreement with the planning model I described. He then makes five significant points that agree with my experience.

1. A unified purpose can be achieved only when all segments of the life of the church see themselves as part of a larger whole with a single goal.

2. Isolated individual decisions and commitments often influence future plans, even when they are not intended to do so.

3. When careful planning is lacking, groups in the church often become competitive with one another and duplicate one another's work.

4. Without coordinated planning, groups in the church may come to feel they are ends in themselves and lose their sense of perspective in relation to the church.

5. Long-range planning is demanded by the magnitude of each church's task. The majority of churches (3, p. 96) in the United States have fewer than 200 active members, according to the data available from major denominations. Most pastors have minimal management education and experience before entering active ministry and want to spend their time performing pastoral functions for which they are trained. Further-

more, few of these churches can or do draw on a pool of lay people with management training or skills. As such, the planning, objective setting, and other management functions are largely neglected.

Planning and objective setting of the strategic long-range type have been largely neglected or purposely avoided by churches. This reluctance to plan stems from the fact that many view the application of long-range planning as inappropriate and unspiritual (50, p. 85). Some have felt that as churches are not businesses, they must not be managed as such. Spiritual management is required for a spiritual organization. According to this view, church leaders are supposed to manage through God's perfect guidance and direction, to wait patiently for God to make things happen rather than "forcing things to happen." Furthermore, churches are admonished to strive for truly spiritual goals, not numerical goals or quantifiable goals stressed in business (37, p. 34).

The need for the performance of managerial functions in churches for them to be more effective ministerially was recognized as early as 1956, according to an article by F. Marvin Myers (37). It was stated that churches would grow faster and be more effective if business managers were hired instead of assistant ministers. In 1956, several church business administrators met in Oklahoma City to share ideas, problems, and solutions, and the following year many more churches sent representatives to the meeting in Dallas, Texas, and the National Association of Church Business Administrators was formed. Vast social questions and complex conditions in almost every community emphasize the need for good management in churches (15, p. 30).

According to Gary Gray (12, p. 42), "Planning in churches without quantitative goals, clearly understood and widely supported, vigorous progress is unlikely and probably impossible."

The importance of goal setting was recognized as providing direction and unity of purpose. The author stressed that it must be the congregation's goal, *as it is not the planners but the congregation* that will ensure the plan's success. However, he reiterated that a balance should be struck and the two mistakes of planning extremes, that of asking the congregation to do either all the thinking or none, be avoided. The importance of planning to bring these objectives to fruition was also emphasized. Planning (12, p. 10) is not easy but the alternative is for the church to be tossed to and fro, buffeted by every unforeseen circumstance and blown off course.

Creative planning is seen as the churches' hope for the future. Visionary thinking, solid purpose, or long-range dream should be first in the basic concern of the church ministry. In a society where many institutions are becoming stagnant, it is imperative that churches have an expanding vision. Church planning has never been met with much enthusiasm. Even in larger churches, the enthusiasm for a plan seldom extends beyond a year unless it involves a new building. However, this basically misunderstood and poorly appreciated planning is, according to one author, a major factor in sharing the hope for the world — the gospel of Christ (28, p. 5).

The level of planning sophistication used by churches seemed to increase as the size of the churches increased. Planning sophistication was more significantly related to the environment than to location, a finding which demonstrates the importance of the leaders' perceptions. The evidence also indicated an appropriate use of planning by churches in the various strategic types. The findings revealed that planning had been used by the churches which had changed strategic types. The findings regarding planning sophistication and growth were not conclusive. Findings regarding the motivations for participation or nonparticipation in long-range planning and the benefits and problems associated with long-range planning were discussed (17). A major contribution to the use of SLRP in churches and ministries has been the Church Growth Movement. This movement began back in 1955 when Dr. Donald A. McGarven published his book, *Bridges of God*. This book eventually became what some have called the "Magna Carta of the Church Growth Movement" (51, p. 23). McGavran has done extensive research in the area of church growth as well as serving in many missionary capacities throughout the world. Because of his contributions to the movement, he has earned the title, "Father of the Church Growth Movement" (51, p. 15). Studying his works is a must for those interested in learning the different concepts of church growth.

McGavran, along with George Hunter III, later wrote *Church Growth Strategies That Work*. This book provides practical ideas for church growth, including strategies of motivating congregations to become more involved in the church. These strategies can easily fit into the planning process in order for a church to set its objectives.

VISIONS AND DREAMS

1

The Church Growth Movement

The Church Growth Movement is more than thirty years old and has made several contributions in the area of church planning. For example, in an article by Win Arn entitled "Understanding and Implementing Growth for Your Church," the author describes what he calls a *Church Growth Development Scale*. In this scale there are eight steps to achieving church growth. As noted, comparisons can be made to the steps of SLRP (as outlined in the introductory chapter of this book) for churches and ministries. The eight steps are as follows: (1, p. 84)

1. Ignorance — no unified direction or sense of mission

2. Information — church members need to be involved

3. Infusion — the need for a dream

4. Individual Change — evaluate present church activity
   — conduct surveys

5. Organization Change — goals reviewed in light of mission priority
   — establish statement of purpose
   — involve laity in setting goals

31

6. Awkward Application — monitor growth projects

      — communicate early success

7. Integration — people feel sense of accomplishment

      — more people becoming involved

8. Innovation — share credit with laity, enlarge dream

      — write book to communicate experiences.

Another major contributor to the church growth movement is C. Peter Wagner. He has written numerous articles and books on this subject. *Church Growth: State of the Art* is one of his more recent works. This book, published in 1986, is a compilation of works written by some of the top people in the field of church growth today. Wagner agrees with a concept I discovered and published in my 1974 book, *MBO: Blue Collar to Top Executive*. Wagner emphasizes the need for a purpose statement as well as dreams and involvement. In this book a wide range of topics are covered, including a glossary of church growth terms, a list of trends among the world's twenty largest churches, and the use of computers in church growth, to name a few.

During the late 1960's and early 1970's, more and more studies were done in the area of church planning. Lyle E. Schaller published several books concerning church management at this time. In 1968 he wrote a book called *The Local Church Looks to the Future: A Guide to Church Planning*. In order to plan for the future, the author stresses the importance of developing a statement of purpose for a church. Areas to include in the statement of purpose are congregational care, outreach and evangelism, and witness and mission (42, p. 33) He feels that the "difference in definition of statement of purpose constitutes the greatest single source of tension in churches" (42, p. 15). Another area discussed was the use of goal setting in order to carry out the purpose. Simply put as a strategy, the author sums this up by stating that a church should go from purpose to program to performance (42, p. 47). This process includes long- and short-range goal setting and provides examples of planning situations encountered in churches.

In 1971, Schaller wrote *Parish Planning*. This book places an emphasis on how to involve the congregation in the planning process, and is more or less considered a sequel to *The Local Church Looks to the Future*. The planning process itself is discussed with emphasis placed in the area of evaluation. Also discussed are ways to transform the planning process so that plans become actual programs in the church. As stated, the most neglected area in the church is evangelism. It is estimated that 60 to 90 percent of the money in churches is spent on ministry to existing members (43, p. 211). The budget needs to be looked at in relation to the objectives that are set during the planning process. I also encourage the budget to be tied into the strategic long-range planning process.

Schaller further developed his studies in the area of church planning and published a book in 1975 entitled *Creative Church Administration*. In this book he describes four planning models. They include "planning from strength," "planning from weakness," "planning by cliche" and "getting from here to there." The last model asks the question, "What is God calling this congregation to be and to do five years from today?" (44, p. 62) This model is similar to the one I use in my planning process. The author and I stress both the process and product in planning. He feels that all who can take a meaningful part should be involved in developing the plan. In discussing this, Schaller gives several steps to developing a plan: (44, p. 131)

1. Develop a purpose, or reason for existence

2. Develop long-term objectives

3. Discover needs within church and community through gathering and analyzing data

4. Isolate concerns

5. Set goals in each of the priority areas, complete with strategies and action plans

6. Open process at all levels for suggestions.

This planning model is similar to mine and includes many of the same steps. The assumptions stage, however, is the main step that is not in this model. Also not included is the reward system as part of the planning process. The author concludes by giving several key questions that should be asked during the evaluation stage of the planning process. They include the following:

1. What is the health of the group life?

— Determine the number of members who belong to a church that has meaning to them.

2. What is the median date?

— Determine the median of membership length and divide the group in two (average is seven to ten years).

3. Who evaluates worship?

— Determine standards for evaluation.

4. What are the rules here?

— Determine parameters of proper conduct.

5. What happened to you?

— Discover experiences that keep members in your church.

In 1975, Norman M. Lambert published *Managing Church Groups.* In this work, the author discusses the importance of goal setting in the church. He shares a model of planning that he calls "Church Management by Objectives and Results" (CMOR). This system "involves a clear and precise identification of what is to be achieved, the establishment of a realistic program for achieving it, and the use of concrete and measurable evidence to evaluate the success of the program" (21, p. 5). The CMOR concept has five steps to planning that include the following: (21, p. 12)

1. Writing a mission statement

   a. broadness of scope

   b. functional commitment

   c. resource commitment

   d. unique or distinctive nature of the work

   e. description of service offered

   f. description of groups served

   g. geographical area covered

2. Developing data for objectives

3. Writing objectives

4. Programming and scheduling (action plans)

5. Allocating resources.

As with some of the other sources reviewed, this book also discusses the other functions of management, including staffing, leading, controlling, and organizing. For the purposes of this research, Lambert has chosen to concentrate on the planning aspects of management. Many people feel this is the foundational function of management.

The Rev. Olan Hendrix wrote the book *Management for the Christian Leader* in 1976. As a consultant and missionary in many parts of the world, the author shares his knowledge concerning the functions of management. In reference to planning, he describes objective setting as one of the most important areas. Hendrix shares four leading questions on objective setting that should be noted: (17, p. 51)

1. What are your objectives?

2. What are your opportunities or open doors?

3. What are your resources?

4. What is your strategy for applying your resources to your opportunities to obtain your objectives?

These questions provide an excellent format to begin the objective-setting stage in the planning process. The author then goes on to say that corporate goals should be set both for the long and short range. After corporate goals are established, individual goals need to be developed. In doing this, you should follow these five rules: (17, p. 55)

1. Consider past performance
2. Set realistic levels
3. Use measurable terms
4. Build in an improvement factor
5. Take people action.

This author supplies the reader with much information on objective setting in relation to the planning process. He also discusses forecasting, policy making, programming, procedures, scheduling, and budgeting. Hendrix writes about these concepts in light of his many endeavors in the Lord's work throughout the world and does well to relate them to the Christian perspectives. As research continued in the area of church management and planning during the late 1970s, more books were published on this topic.

In 1977, Alvin Lindgren wrote a book entitled *Management for Your Church*. This author discusses mission statement and environmental analysis. The most important area the author writes about, however, refers to the five organizational theories and their characteristics. This is especially important when trying to understand the different management styles in churches. A portion of the chart from this book is given here to provide the reader a framework to understand these concepts (24, p. 26).

1. Traditional — Made by elders, unhurried pace
   — Assumed, seldom articulated

2. Charismatic — Spontaneous, unpredictable
   — Explicit, reflect aim of leader

3. Classical   — Orders from the top,
                      rationalized, calculated
               — Objective and quantitative

4. Human Relations — Group decision
                      — Subjective, purposes of
                      group emerge

5. Systems   — Adapt with purpose relevant to
                   environment
               — Definitive, unifying; consider
                   environment

These organizational theories are important when comparisons are made of different churches and their leaders. This present study hopes to build on such models as the one from Lindgren's book. It will also provide further research into the areas of church planning based upon research previously written, as well as analysis of new data collected by the author.

In 1978, Robert N. Gray wrote *Managing the Church: Business Administration.* Included in volume one is "the church in relation to its management functions." Several key points are made concerning church planning. The author describes ten principles in this area (13, p. 65).

1. Primacy — planning is viewed as the primary function in the managerial process, and should include objective setting.

2. Alternatives — ways to best serve the congregation in light of available resources.

3. Objectives — planning process begins with a defined mission and objectives.

4. Contribution to mission — all plans of activity need to be evaluated by their contribution to mission.

5. Maximum involvement — need input from all members.

6. Work simplification — find one best way of doing something.

7. Waste reduction — program of cost and waste reduction needs to be in effect.

8. Value analysis — maximize resources of church.

9. Flexibility — plans need to be flexible.

10. Directional change — unanticipated events may cause a change in direction.

These ten principles outlined by Gray are, in essence, the areas I address in my planning system. They come together to form a list of some of the benefits of a strategic long-range planning system.

Dale McConkey, a longtime friend and professional associate, published a book in 1978 by the name of *Goal Setting: A Guide to Achieving the Church's Mission*. This booklet is from the *Administrative Series for Churches*. When the series is taken together it makes up a church administrative handbook. This particular booklet has proved to be one of the most complete, as well as one of the easiest to understand, of the books researched for this study. It lists ten steps in the goal-setting process. They are similar to my model and are as follows: (26, p. 17)

1. Determine church's mission

2. Select key result areas

3. Complete situational analysis

    a. strengths

    b. weaknesses

      c. opportunities

      d. threats

4. Establish overall church objectives

5. Enunciate overall church objectives to congregation

6. Members write individual goals

7. Program (plan) individual goals

8. Consolidate all goals and plans

9. Establish feedback methods to measure progress

10. Repeat each year.

This model has obvious direct comparisons to my model. Assumptions are not discussed in this model. Also not discussed is the way in which the review process can be tied into the reward system. McConkey is helpful again in the objectives chapter later in the text.

Charles Wilson wrote the book entitled *Principles and Procedures in Performance Evaluation: Part I With the Performance Evaluation Kit* (60). This book was also published in 1978 and is designed to aid the church leader with a tool to use in performance evaluation that is not complex and can be used without outside help. It needs to be read along with the other books in the kit. Overall, it provides the reader with ways in which performance appraisal can be administered in a church setting. The six points to evaluation are:

1. Formation and focusing of the group
   — determine areas of accountability to be covered
   — determine if group members are comfortable with tasks

40

2. Calibration of the group
   — determine standards of performance for each person
   — determine if each person agrees to these standards

3. The evaluation
   — What is actually happening?

4. Information learned
   — What has been learned from step three?

5. The future
   — explore ideas for feedback in the future

6. The debriefing
   — thank group for their help, break out of roles, and close meetings.

It should be noted, however, that performance appraisal can, at best, end up being a subjective exercise by the employee and the employer. To avoid this, performance appraisal needs to be tied into the planning process. I stress this in a later chapter of this book.

Richard Hutcheson, Jr. published *Wheel Within the Wheel* in 1979 (20). In this book, the author discusses management techniques and organizational methods in the church. He writes about this subject in light of his work with the Presbyterian Church. The book deals with the spiritual aspects of a church in terms of its organizational methods. Hutcheson then discusses different management systems.

Within this context, the author talks about the effects of management techniques on the church. The history of the mission of the church is discussed. As described by the author, a pre-1945 definition of the word "mission" would be religious and read as follows:

"The act of sending, or state of being sent with certain powers, especially to propagate religion" (20, p. 69).

As time progressed, the word *mission* was transformed into the plural to include the missionary emphasis in the world. In essence, mission should include the goals of the church.

The author also evaluates MBO and its applications to the church in planning. In doing this, goal setting is discussed as it is broken down into objectives and strategies. The most important contribution of this book, however, is contained in the last chapter. Here the author declares that the most basic organizational principle is trust in the Holy Spirit. This needs to override all functions in the church. As summed up at the end of the book, the author states the following:

> Balance is essential. Trusting the Holy Spirit does not mean neglecting management and maintenance. Trusting the Spirit means, among other things, counting on the Spirit to provide good managers, to redeem organizational techniques, to work through Christian people in bureaucracies — even through their manipulations, their politics, their tinkering. But it always means to recognize that God is the ultimate manager (20, p. 228).

In 1980, *Key Steps in Local Church Planning* was written by a group of authors. The planning model outlined in this book includes five interlocking steps: (11, p. 13)

1. Purpose — review what church is called to be and to become

2. Goal development — developing goals and objectives based on purpose and data about your church, community and world

3. Mission design — design program plans to achieve objectives

4. Mission management — doing ministry of church based on program plan details (MBO)

5. Mission evaluation — what you intended to do versus what you actually did.

This manual provides an excellent foundation for understanding the concepts of planning in churches. It supplies the reader with an easy-to-understand, step-by-step process for planning. The outcome of this is to turn plans into results. This is done through committee format. The book outlines a way in which committees can be utilized in developing a plan for a church.

Robert White published a book, *Managing Today's Church*, in 1981. In chapter two, he discussed the strategic planning process as it applies to the church. He outlined a seven-step process that includes the following: (58, p. 25)

1. Analysis of the external environment

2. Analysis of internal capabilities

3. Determination of opportunities and threats, strengths and weaknesses, key issues

4. Setting objectives

5. Selecting strategies which enable you to achieve your objectives

6. Developing action plans (tactics)

7. Determining the budget.

White also briefly discussed performance appraisal and how it relates to the planning process and the reward system. He is one of the few who describes how to tie these areas together. Overall, his book is excellent in providing the reader with management theories and techniques that cover a wide range of topics faced by a pastor in day-to-day dealings in the church.

In 1984, Douglas Walrath wrote *Planning for Your Church* (52). Walrath stressed the use of basic planning as the key to the success of the planning process. He emphasized the role of the congregation in planning and described ways to organize programs in order to fulfill the goals set for the church. The author feels that every church needs to have a planning committee. Once this is set up, internal and external analysis should take place. Committees need to have what the author described as a "church checkup." In doing this, overall trends, demographics, and financial analysis need to be done. This procedure corresponds to my "strengths and weaknesses" phase of planning.

His external analysis includes a community update, which involves defining your own territory. This step compares with my "environmental analysis." Usually, territorial boundaries are defined in the purpose statement. Walrath also discussed the use of surveys in planning. He suggested community interviews as one means of administering surveys. If the church has access to the resources and expertise to take such surveys, valuable information can be obtained. As a summary, the basic planning process involves seven steps: (52, p. 105)

1. Data-gathering by task forces
2. Conference with planning committee
3. Preparing proposals
4. Approval by policy board(s)
5. Preparing action plan
6. Approval by policy board(s)
7. Implementation.

This seven-step process addresses one way in which planning systems can operate under a church structure with a board. The key point here is that in order to implement a plan, one must be operating with objectives and not mere ideas. As the author states, an objective is "something specific to be achieved by a certain person or group within a definite period of time" (52, p. 105).

Charles Tidwell made a contribution to church planning during the same year when he wrote *Church Administration: Effective Leadership for Ministry.* This book set up a management system that includes several key areas: (49, p. 58)

1. Clarify purpose
2. Determine objectives
3. Develop ministry plans
4. Design organization
5. Administer human resources
6. Administer physical resources
7. Administer financial resources
8. Provide controls.

The author also included an argument for the use of planning in churches. Tidwell listed the benefits of planning, as well as the implementation of the planning process. Planning, however, is but one subject discussed. Tidwell addressed the complexities of church administration and supplied the reader with many scriptural references to support the concepts he presents.

Another contributor to church planning is Dr. Larry Lea. In 1985, he wrote a book entitled *Mending Broken Nets and Broken Fishermen* (22). In this book, Lea shared his experiences as pastor of one of the fastest-growing churches in America today. In chapter eight, Lea discussed the concept of goal-oriented leadership. He believes this is the key to church growth. Lea stated the following concerning goal-oriented leadership:

> . . . When I speak of restoring goal-oriented leadership, I am not referring to "hype," positive mental attitude or man-made and man-motivated objectives; rather, I am referring to Spirit-imparted goals and Spirit-empowered fishermen (22, p. 119).

He then went on to proclaim that the restoration of this type of leadership is absolutely essential for a church to grow both spiritually and numerically. Lea believes if a church does not have goals, stagnation will set in. In order to set these goals, however, Lea stresses the reliance on the Holy Spirit. He gives the reader a balanced view of goal-setting and planning. A pastor should not plan based upon set formulas from a book. He should not be so sophisticated that he forgets to rely on the Holy Spirit. Every goal needs to be birthed by the Spirit, Lea stated, for God's glory.

Lea's book is essential reading for any pastor or church leader who is serious about keeping the fish in the boat once they are caught. (Note my further analysis of his work in the last chapter of this book.)

The Rev. Robert H. Schuller is another pastor who has contributed significantly to the church growth movement. His book, *Your Church Has a Fantastic Future* (45), addressed seven key principles for a successful church along with eleven attitudes that hinder growth. The success principles are:

1. Accessibility — churches should be easy to find

2. Surplus parking — *more than enough* parking

3. Inventory — enough programs to meet needs

4. Service — recruit, train, and motivate lay people

5. Visibility — churches should be in the public eye

6. Possibility thinking — asking the right questions, thinking strategically

7. Good cash flow — managing your money and others.

The eleven attitudes Schuller listed as hindering growth are:

1. Church growth just happens

2. Detachment from the world

3. Boredom

4. Negative emotions

5. Denominational success

6. Fear of debt

7. Lack of conviction

8. Distraction from primary mission

9. The controversial pulpit

10. Shortsighted leadership

11. Impossibility thinking.

Schuller provided the reader with a list of key points he learned through his years of service as a pastor and as a motivational speaker. These principles should be studied and prayed about by any pastor who is serious about church growth. (Note in Appendix H that I have analyzed these factors as they pertain to several churches.)

As stated previously, one school of thought believes planning and objective setting is essential for churches to operate in the future.

It has often been said by many, "If you do not know where you are going, any road will take you there."

Dr. Paul Yonggi Cho, pastor of the largest church in the world, believes every pastor needs a vision or a dream. He stated at a conference at Oral Roberts University in 1986, "Visions and dreams are the vessels through which your desires are fulfilled." He then went on to say that "without a specific goal, a vision is no vision." Many leaders describe Cho as one of the great goal-oriented pastors of our time. The evidence of this can be seen by the number of people who attend his church. He has an active membership roll of more than 500,000 people. His next major goal is to reach ten million Japanese with the gospel of Jesus Christ. This is an example of a man who operates on the basis of planning for the future by setting goals, and then striving to reach them.

Planning has received more and more recognition in the area of its applicability to churches, yet there are some who doubt its worth to a religious organization. An article in *Christian Leadership Letter* states the following:

> Many people are "Antiplanner," not just passively, but actively! . . . But once we begin to see that for the Christian, planning is making statements of faith about what God wants us to do and be, the Antiplanners may become converts (5, pp. 1,3).

Cho, for example, is ridiculed by some for setting numeric goals. This does not seem to be "religious" to some. It appears to be too "businesslike," and often it is believed that the pastor is taking on the world's standards if he operates using business skills that have been applied to the secular world. Cho responds to this by quoting the following scripture found in Proverbs 29:18: **Where there is no vision, the people perish.** He then proclaims, "If you will show me your vision, I will prophesy your future" (48, pp. 44-46). In essence, a person's plans for the future will determine where that person will be.

What does the Bible say about planning? I believe the Holy Spirit helps us know God's will and actions that are anointed. We do our best, then ask God for His best. My spirit confirms when the right plan is in the will of God. Nothing in this book is meant to imply that the Lord is to be left out. Proverbs 20:5 says, "A plan in the heart of man is like deep water" (paraphrased). Luke 14:28 states, "For which one of you when he wants to build a tower does not sit down and calculate the cost?" (paraphrased).

> Through wisdom is an house builded; and by understanding it is established.
>
> Proverbs 24:3
>
> For God is not the author of confusion, but of peace. . . .
>
> 1 Corinthians 14:33
>
> Let all things be done decently and in order.
>
> 1 Corinthians 14:40

In Proverbs, much instruction is given on preparing for the future.

> Plans fail for lack of counsel, but with many advisors they succeed.
>
> Commit to the Lord whatever you do, and your plans will succeed.
>
> In his heart a man plans his course, but the Lord determines his steps.
>
> The plans of the diligent lead to profit as surely as haste leads to poverty.
>
> Proverbs 15:22; 16:3,9; 20:3 NIV

Psalm 20:4 says:

> May he give you the desire of your heart and make all your plans succeed.

A careful study of the Bible demonstrates the appropriateness and necessity of planning for the believer in his daily affairs. We attempted to establish in the introduction that:

1) methods used successfully in industry are applicable to churches and ministries; 2) a number of church leaders and authors believe there is a place for better planning and management; 3) pastors surveyed believe overwhelmingly there is a need for strategic planning; 4) most of the identifiable failures cannot be

blamed on the devil, and 5) the Bible supports, overall, a growing sense of that concept. Note the following verses:

Purpose, Mission, Vision

Proverbs 11:14:	"For lack of guidance a nation (or in our case 'a person') falls, but many advisers make victory sure." (NIV)
Proverbs 15:22:	"Plans fail for lack of counsel, but with many advisers they succeed." (NIV)
Proverbs 20:18:	"Every purpose is established by counsel . . . ."
Proverbs 16:20:	"He that handleth a matter wisely shall find good . . . ."
Proverbs 29:18:	"Where there is no vision, the people perish . . ."
Proverbs 23:7:	"As a man thinketh in his heart, so is he" (paraphrased).
Joel 2:28:	". . . Your old men shall dream dreams, your young men shall see visions."
Acts 2:17:	(Essentially the same as Joel 2:28.)
Romans 12:3:	"For by the grace given me I say to every one of you: Do not think of yourself more highly than you ought, but rather think of yourself with sober judgment, in accordance with the measure of faith God has given you." (NIV)

Galatians 6:34:   "If anyone thinks he is something when he is nothing, he deceives himself. Each one should test his own actions. Then he can take pride in himself, without comparing himself to somebody else . . . ." (NIV)

Ephesians 4:1:   ". . . I urge you to live a life worthy of the calling you have received" (NIV).

Psalm 37:4:   "Delight yourself in the Lord and he will give you the desires of your heart" (NIV).

Matthew 6:33:   "But seek first his kingdom and his righteousness, and all these things will be given to you as well" (NIV).

Environmental Analysis

Proverbs 25:2:   "It is the glory of God to conceal a thing: but the honour of kings is to search out a matter."

Strengths and Weaknesses

Luke 12:48:   "To whom much is given, much is required" (paraphrased).

2 Timothy 3:17:   ". . . Complete and proficient, well-fitted and thoroughly equipped for every good work" (AMP).

Objectives

Nehemiah 2:4:   "For what dost thou make request? . . ." (What do you want?)

Strategy

Matthew 5:15:   "Neither do people light a lamp and put it under a bowl. Instead they put it on its stand, and it gives light to everyone in the house" (paraphrased).

Operational Plan

2 Timothy 2:15:   "Study to shew thyself approved unto God, a workman that needeth not to be ashamed . . . ."

2 Timothy 3:17:   ". . . Complete and proficient, well-fitted and thoroughly equipped for every good work" (AMP).

Luke 14:28:   "For which one of you when he wants to build a tower does not sit down and calculate the cost?" (paraphrased).

James 1:23:   "For if any be a hearer of the word, and not a doer, he is like unto a man beholding his natural face in a glass."

1 Corinthians 14:40: "Let all things be done decently and in order."

1 Corinthians 16:9: "For a great door and effectual is opened unto me, and there are many adversaries."

Philippians 4:13: "I can do all things through Christ which strengtheneth me."

Colossians 3:17: "And whatsoever ye do in word or deed, do all in the name of the Lord Jesus . . . ."

Proverbs 16:9: "We should make plans — counting on God to direct us." (TLB)

Proverbs 16:3: "Commit thy works unto the Lord . . . ."

Colossians 3:23: "Whatever you do, work at it with all your heart, as working for the Lord, not for men" (NIV).

Nehemiah 2:4: ". . . For what dost thou make request? So I prayed to the God of heaven."

Plan in General

Proverbs 15:22: "Plans fail for lack of counsel, but with many advisers they succeed" (NIV).

Proverbs 16:10: "A divine sentence is in the lips of the king: his mouth transgresseth not in judgment."

Proverbs 19:20: "Hear counsel and receive instruction, that thou mayest be wise . . . ."

Proverbs 20:5:   "A plan in the heart of a man is like deep water" (paraphrased).

Proverbs 24:3:   "Through wisdom is an house builded; and by understanding it is established."

1 Corinthians 14:33: "For God is not the author of confusion, but of peace . . . ."

Reward

1 Corinthians 3:8: "Now he who plants and he who waters are one; but each will receive his own reward according to his own labor" (paraphrased).

Proverbs 13:21:   ". . . The righteous will be rewarded with prosperity" (paraphrased).

Philippians 3:14:   "I press toward the mark for the prize of the high calling of God in Christ Jesus."

The following chapter covers each step of the planning process. The theory behind each step is presented, and actual examples are given to help understand that step. Make notes on your own situation as you read. Read on with excitement.

"...objectives and resources [can] rest on shaky foundations."

2
Defining Your Purpose

The first and probably most important consideration when developing a long-range plan with this new definition of MBO is to define the purpose, mission, or the "reason for being" for the organization or any specific part of it. This is usually a difficult process. Oral Roberts and Peter Drucker are the key influences in the logic that led me to put purpose as the first step. When I read Drucker's *Management: Tasks, Responsibilities, and Practice* in 1974, I became convinced that purpose had to be the key. During the past few years I have seen the importance of visions and dreams in the purpose statement. Drucker (7, p. 79), in discussing the importance of identifying an organization's purpose, starts with the marketing concept, which is to organize a business to satisfy a need in the marketplace.

He says, "It is defined by the want the customer satisfies when he buys a product or a service. To satisfy the customer is the mission and purpose of every business" (7, p. 79). He adds:

Business enterprise, however, requires that the theory of the business be thought through and spelled out. It demands a clear definition of business purpose and business mission. It raises the questions, "What is our business, and what should it be?" (7, p. 75)

In my books, *MBO: Blue Collar to Top Executive, An MBO Approach to Long-Range Planning, Develop a Strategic Plan for Your Life,* and *Strategic Long-Range Planning,* I emphasized that many steps must be considered before setting objectives. The purpose is listed first in my definition largely because of the influence of Oral Roberts. When I was on the Oral Roberts University faculty, I saw the value of constant recognition of purpose and "reason for being" when evaluating plans for the future.

Dr. Richard Johanson is a leader in recognizing the importance of the pre-objectives-setting stage. He began developing this concept at Continental-Emsco Company in the 1950s. Drucker declares:

> Only a clear definition of the mission and purpose of the business makes possible clear and realistic business objectives. It is the foundation for priorities, strategies, plans and work assignments. It is the starting point for the design of managerial jobs and, above all, for the design of managerial structures (7, p. 75).

> Clearly, if purpose is defined casually or introspectively, or the list of key result areas neglects some of the less obvious threats and opportunities, the fabric of organization objectives and resources rests on shaky foundations. As Calvin Coolidge put it: "No enterprise can exist for itself alone. It ministers to some great need, it performs some great service not for itself but for others; or failing therein it ceases to be profitable and ceases to exist" (19, p. 19).

It is not always easy to formulate a statement of purpose. Drucker describes how American Telephone & Telegraph Company defined its business purpose:

> Our business is service. This sounds obvious once it has been said. But first there had to be the realization that a telephone system, being a natural monopoly, was susceptible to nationalization and that a privately owned telephone service in a developed and industrialized country was exceptional and needed community support for its survival. Second, there had to be the realization that community support could not be obtained by propaganda campaigns or by attacking crisis as "unAmerican" or "socialistic." It could be obtained only by creating customer satisfaction (7, p. 77).

The purpose statement should have the dream and vision of what the organization wants to be. Members should try to visualize what they want the organization to be. If they can see where they are going and have an image of the real mission of the organization, their plans will fall more easily into place.

A *statement of purpose* prescribed by the board of directors of an organized church might be:

> To foster renewed spiritual direction and growth to meet the need for meaningful worship on behalf of congregational laymen at large.

It is in this purpose statement that the vision and the dream for the church or ministry must be reflected. This purpose statement sets the stage for all planning.

Objectives, which are covered later in the text, must by their very nature contribute to achieving what is in the purpose statement.

In a study of private Christian college and university administrations, we found all surveyed had a purpose and mission statement, but only 50 percent had specific measurable objectives of what was to be accomplished.

Tulsa Christian Fellowship, a nondenominational church in Tulsa, has used this brand of MBO. It took six weeks of hard work for the elders to agree on a statement of purpose. Developing a purpose statement is not an easy task!

Dr. James Buskirk and his staff at First United Methodist in Tulsa developed and updated their purpose statement in January 1987. Dr. Buskirk then wove the draft of the purpose statement into a January sermon. This is a good way to introduce to the congregation that long-range planning is taking place. Also, it is a good idea to ask the congregation for input into the purpose statement. A number of churches have followed my advice and then either made it available on a typed sheet or put the draft of the purpose statement into the church newspaper and bulletin. The key is to emphasize that it is a draft, and that suggestions are encouraged. I even suggest writing the word "draft" across the top somewhere. If the posted statement looks too neat and tidy, people get the idea that is the final draft and will not respond as readily with suggestions.

World Visions' June 1984 *Christian Leadership Letter* lists seven reasons to have a mission statement:

First, it gives us a reason for being, an explanation to ourselves and others as to why we exist as an organization.

Second, the mission statement helps us to place boundaries around our ministry and thus define what we will do and what we will not do.

Third, a mission statement describes the need we are attempting to meet in the world.

Fourth, a mission statement gives a general description of how we are going to respond to that need.

Fifth, a mission statement acts as the hook on which the primary objectives of the organization can be hung.

Sixth, a mission statement helps to form the basis for the ethos (or culture) of the organization.

Seventh, a mission statement helps us to communicate to those outside the organization what we are all about (34, pp. 1,2).

Norman M. Lambert, in his book *Managing Church Groups* (21, p. 28), gives helpful tips on writing and evaluating a purpose statement. Some I feel especially important are:

1. Identify the mission of that part of the organization to which the group is accountable. A parish council may be accountable to the parish at large, the pastor, bishop, diocesan pastoral council, or all of these. The liturgy committee will be accountable to the parish council. The director of religious education may be accountable to the religious education committee, pastor, or both.

2. Determine that portion of the above mission statement for which the group is accountable. While the parish council is accountable for the total parish operation, the maintenance committee, for example, will be responsible only for that portion of the parish council's mission that deals with maintaining the grounds and buildings in a usable and functional state.

3. Prepare a rough draft of the mission statement that covers the purpose of the group and the major activities it performs. With a working team, such as a parish staff or parish council, a rough draft mission statement can be developed at an all-day meeting, using an outside facilitator who is familiar with communications techniques, group process, and the concept of mission statements. The meeting can begin with each individual writing his own version of the mission statement on newsprint. When these drafts are all assembled, the group can review each one for clarity and understanding, applying the *Questions for Evaluating Mission Statements*. Finally, condense those portions that are similar so that only areas of wide disagreement are left. At this point, negotiations can be carried out between members of the group until there is general agreement on all points ("I am able to live with this"). The final result is the rough draft of the mission statement.

Basic Factors of the Mission Statement

1. Broadness of scope and continuity of application:

The statement should be broad enough to cover all significant areas of activity expected of the organization without a specific termination period indicated.

2. Functional commitment:

The nature of the work, tasks or activities to be performed must be described in terms that will determine clearly the validity of the group or organization.

3. Resource commitment:

The statement should include a commitment to cost-effective utilization of available resources.

4. Unique or distinctive nature of work:

Every unit in an organization should make some unique or at least distinctive contribution. If there are two or more peer units in an organization with identical mission statements, the risk of duplicated effort is obvious.

5. Description of services to be offered.

6. Description of group or groups to be served.

7. Geographical area to be covered.

Questions for Evaluating Mission Statements

1. Does it contain all important commitments?

2. Does it clearly state the function?

3. Is there a clear determination of relationships to the rest of the organization?

4. Is it distinct from the mission statements of other groups in the organization?

5. Is it short, to the point and understandable?

6. Is it continuing in nature?

7. Does it state to whom the group is accountable?

Jim Durkin published a book called the *Master Builder* in 1985. Included in this work is a series of chapters covering foundational concepts for the local church. Durkin addresses several key issues concerning planning. The first deals with the idea of purpose and vision. It is important to understand this concept in order to have a successful church. As the author states, the vision is what unites the body of believers together. Durkin then goes on to discuss the idea of building a church with a long-term plan. He relates this style of managing to flying a plane, and goes on to proclaim:

> A church without a long-term perspective will follow the same pattern. Instead of moving with steadiness and certainty toward God's goals, it will continually swerve off course. It will be caught up with every wind of doctrine that blows through . . . There is an endless supply of distractions that will take a church off the course of pursuing God's purpose and vision (9, p. 45).

This chapter in Durkin's book is a must for a group developing a mission statement. It is the best guide I have found to date.

Generally a purpose statement can reflect whether the church wants to be local, regional, national or international, profit or nonprofit, needs to be met, and so forth. I like the word "service" included in the mission statement of any organization.

The purpose statement needs to answer the question of why your church and ministry are needed in the first place. Plenty of others exist. Discuss and know specifically what need you are meeting.

Lyle E. Schaller, in his book *The Local Church Looks to the Future*, states that a purpose statement needs to be built around these points:

1. *Congregational Care* — typically this includes corporate worship, administration of the sacraments, pastoral care, fellowship and the nurturing, education and training for Christian discipleship of the members.

2. *Outreach and Evangelism* — this part of the statement focuses on the imperative to go out and confront individuals outside the church with the good news that Jesus Christ is their Redeemer and Savior. While the first part of this outline was directed toward the parish's ministry to persons inside the gathered community, this part of the outline emphasizes the parish's responsibility to individuals outside the church.

3. *Witness and Mission* — the emphasis here is on the church's responsibility to be a living witness to Christ in the world to the groups, organizations, structures, and institutions outside the church in the world. This also helps the members to understand both the legitimacy and the imperative for the parish's involvement in the social, economic and political issues in the local community. (42, p. 33)

For example, Victory Christian Center in Tulsa determined it was a local church with an international outreach. Morris Cerullo World Evangelism, based in

San Diego, is truly an international ministry. Victory and World Evangelism are quite different, but their primary reason for being is the same.

The Bible explicitly admonished us to have a dream and vision. Proverbs 29:18 says, **Where there is no vision, the people perish.** Joel 2:28 says, **Your old men shall dream dreams, your young men shall see visions.** Acts 2:17 says essentially the same thing.

The vision for what something can be creates the spark and energy for the whole planning and management process. It is important to spend time defining this purpose statement with ample emphasis on getting everyone involved in the dream of how things can be. Without a vision, people just work day-to-day and tend not to be as productive or willing to go all out.

In an established denominational church, the focal purpose statement must reflect the support of the overall church statement of purpose. For example, a local Methodist church purpose statement should reflect the overall beliefs and doctrine of the United Methodist Church. John Wesley declared *The Nature, Design and General Rules of the United Societies*, (54) written in 1743, and *Explanatory Notes Upon the New Testament*, (53) written in 1754, are guides for Methodist Biblical exegesis and doctrinal interpretation. In his "Model Deed," written in 1763, he outlined that no Methodist pastor preach doctrine other than that contained in *Notes Upon the New Testament* (55) and the four volumes of *Sermons* (57). The aim was to provide a broad and flexible framework. Wesley's own statement of the purpose of a Methodist Society is described in the *Rules* (56) as:

A company — united in order to pray together, to receive the word of exhortation, and to watch over one another in love, that they may help each other to work out their salvation.

For example, as Dr. James Buskirk of Tulsa First United Methodist Church led his staff through this planning process with my assistance, we all had to be constantly aware of the basic Methodist beliefs to be sure the purpose statement reflected those beliefs. This does not mean that the First United Methodist Church of Tulsa does not have the freedom of a Victory Christian or Calvary Temple to have a vision and dream. It just means they had to be conscious of their roots to remain consistent.

A good statement of purpose not only clarifies what the church does, it sets boundaries. It defines what the church will not do. It helps limit expectations, and that alone can make it the pastor's best friend (46).

NOW DEVELOP A PURPOSE STATEMENT

"...Man really ha no idea
what things will be l e in the future..."

3

Monitoring the Environment

It is vital for the church to gauge the environment within which it operates. This should be standard practice for all churches. My own experience and study have convinced me of the importance of realizing that anything that can happen ultimately will happen. The late Ed Green stated in a long-range planning seminar at ORU that "Man really has no idea what things will be like in the future in spite of our attempts to predict the same." To emphasize the point, could any of us have foreseen in 1963 that within the next twelve years the following portentous events would take place?

1. The United States would have virtually lost its first war.

2. A president would be assassinated.

3. Another president, the first in the United States to do so, would resign from office.

4. A vice president would resign.

5. A president and vice president not elected by the people would be in office.

These events are telling us that we are, in effect, managing change. The only way we can manage change is to constantly monitor the environment within which we operate. Examples for business might be the trends we see in gross national product, governmental control, regulation, the labor movement, interest rates, consumer preference, and so forth.

This environmental analysis stage is where we look at the past, identify trends and, in effect, take the pulse of the environment in which the organization operates. Environmental analysis should not be confused with an assumption base which will be discussed later.

Industry surveys, marketing research, Dow Jones Stock Averages and recent commodity prices are all environmental factors. At Continental Can Company's Chicago Stockyard plant, we watched the pork prices as a signal for demand for ham cans.

An example of environmental analysis might be:

1. "In August 1984, cable penetration was estimated at 42.9 percent of American television households by the Nielsen service, with 36.1 million of the 83.3 million homes with television now having cable. Arbitron's estimates show U.S. Cable penetration to stand at 41 percent, or 34.5 million households." (*Charisma*, April 1985, p. 74, "Cable Connections for Christ.")

2. "Pat Robertson, president of Christian Broadcasting Network (CBN), quoted Cable Age (May 28, 1984) that eleven million subscribers who have access to CBN are watching it in a given week." (*Charisma*, April 1984, p. 74, "Cable Connections for Christ.")

3. "Research by the American Resource Bureau indicates that the total, unduplicated audience for religious programs is about ten million people, or roughly 10 percent of the adult viewing public." (*Charisma*, April 1985, p. 75, "Cable Connections for Christ.")

4. "There are currently more than sixty syndicated religious programs broadcast, and dozens more that do not qualify for syndicated status and measurement." (*Charisma*, April 1985, p. 75, "Cable Connections for Christ.")

5. ". . . Twenty-four-hour Christian satellite networks deliver programming to cable stations across the United States." (*Charisma*, April 1985, p. 75, "Cable Connections for Christ.")

6. "Like so much of its work, the church may be learning that cable television must be a local ministry if it is to be evangelistically effective." (Charisma, April 1985, p. 76, "Cable Connections for Christ.")

7. "Most of the mass media ministries are used for education and growth, reaching the already churched. But in local neighborhoods, cable television has proven to be an effective witness for converting the unsaved to Christ." (*Charisma*, April 1985, p. 76, "Cable Connections for Christ.")

8. "Cable television is one of the best methods of extending the walls of the church and enlarging the outreach of its ministry into (the) local community," writes Lou Schierbeck, station manager of Grace TV, in *Religious Broadcasting* magazine." (*Charisma*, April 1985, p. 76, "Cable Connections for Christ.")

9. "We have found television to be a tremendous public relations tool. Many churches today never have any influence in their community. Many are nonexistent as far as their community is concerned . . . they have no voice, influence or even contact with those outside their fellowship." (*Charisma*, April 1985, p. 77, "Cable Connections for Christ.")

10. "Ministry via cable television — when it is coupled with a local church — allows viewers the opportunity to participate in a non-threatening manner." (*Charisma*, April 1985, p. 77, "Cable Connections for Christ.")

11. In its first fifty years the Pentecostal movement had grown to around ten million worldwide. But in the next thirty-five years (1950-1985), it began to explode, soaring to more than 190 million Pentecostals and Charismatics today.

12. The Assemblies of God is the largest classical Pentecostal denomination in the world. Between 1975 and 1985, the number of worldwide members and adherents has grown from 4,594,780 to 13,175,751 — an increase of 296 percent.

13. Independent Charismatic churches are currently the fastest-growing segment of American religion. (*Ministries Today*, May/June 1987, p. 78, "Where the Action Is," by C. Peter Wagner)

It is important to build a data base. The congregation or partner base can be studied. The more you know about the people being served, the better you can meet that need. Many successful businesses, such as Sears, are continually doing research to learn more about their customers. A ministry should do the same thing. Information can be gathered on: family size, marital status, age levels, where people work, people's needs, how long have members been in the congregation, do people own or rent, where do they live. All of these are good questions to ask and know.

For example, Victory Christian developed a profile of the congregation using modern market research techniques. They found:

53 percent are under age 35, 48 percent have been attending Victory one year or less, 52 percent live within five miles of the church, 31 percent are single, 8 percent are single parents, and so forth.

In a large-scale study in progress on people and their lives, I recently found that of those respondents who were seniors and graduate students at a major Christian University and who also came from a broken home, 56 percent said they had a vision or dream for their lives, while 86 percent from normal homes had a vision for their lives. Of this group, 64.9 percent reported they had specific measurable objectives as to where they wanted to be in five years. A total of 87.4 percent reported they had shared a dream for their lives with someone.

The Church and Community Survey Workbook, published by Convention Press, Nashville, Tennessee, does a good job describing how to conduct good surveys. The book may be purchased (or special ordered) from local Baptist bookstores. The book contains sample questions and many fine ideas. It is a must for anyone involved in serious church or ministry planning. A complete study of the church's emphasis of products, management, policies, and procedures is needed. Also included in this environmental analysis is a study of the management system. The management questionnaire gives management information on the effectiveness of the management system and brings major problems to the surface.

In Robert N. White's book, *Managing Today's Church*, he suggests seven factors to evaluate in this area: (58, p. 25)

1. Economic trends in your locality, in your geographic region, and in the nation (Examples of these trends are changes in personal income, employment, land values, and industry location.)

2. Demographic trends — including shifts in age groups, education levels, numbers of widows and retired people, and shift of population to different geographic area

3. In your community — issues of urban versus suburban development, growth or decline of commercial activities, transportation facilities

4. Also in your community — changes in the services offered to people (Who is offering them? Are services primarily shifting into governmental hands or private sponsorship? How effective are these services in meeting the needs of the community?)

5. Trends in competition for "prime-time" Sunday mornings and evenings and perhaps weekday evenings (What other things are going on that present you with competition for that time?)

6. Church attendance trends in the community and region and reasons for changes in these trends (What activities in churches are proving to be the most popular at this time?)

7. Changes in social values (What do people in your community look on as being important? Is churchgoing an important value? Evaluation in this area can lead into issues such as the strength of family relationships, attitudes toward moral values, and so forth.)

At the company level, another step in a thorough analysis is a complete audit of the organization. Of the various audits, the best I have seen is the "General

Survey Outline" done by McKinsey in his 1922 book, *Budget Control*.

One of the latest pieces of work in terms of a planning audit has been done by Thomas H. Naylor of Duke University. Naylor has developed a questionnaire, called "The Planning Audit," which is a method for auditing the planning system. The work reviews the planning environment, organizational structure, management philosophy and style, planning process, and other factors relating to the organization. The result is a thorough understanding of the planning system. The data collected in the audit can then be analyzed to determine strengths and weaknesses in the planning system. The most important are then included in the strengths-and-weaknesses part of the planning process. Whereas Naylor's work is an audit of only the planning system, James O. McKinsey's work, as mentioned earlier, is a complete audit of the organization.

I developed, with Jeff Horvath's assistance, the audit of a planning/MBO system shown below. McKinsey wrote the "General Survey Outline" to accomplish many of the same things as the outline. By comparison, however, his outline is more comprehensive and detailed. If an organization has the time and resources to go through the "General Survey Outline," it will achieve advantages over Naylor's shorter analysis. At this stage, the organization is set for making assumptions.

Audit — Planning and Management Systems
Sections
   I. Purpose

      A. Is it written?

B. Define boundaries within which your ministry operates.

C. Define the need(s) that your ministry is attempting to meet.

D. Define the market that your ministry is reaching.

E. Do you intend to have local, regional, national, or international scope?

F. Has there been input from others?

G. Does it include the word "service," or a word with similar meaning?

II. Environmental Analysis

A. List several international/national trends that affect your ministry.

B. List several local trends that affect your ministry.

C. List several trends unique to your ministry:
   1. Membership
   2. Active and inactive members
   3. Average attendance at various services
   4. How many baptized, deaths, new members, transfers, and so forth
   5. Sunday School attendance.

D. List several of your most important competitors.
   1. Which are growing, which are declining?

II. Strengths and Weaknesses

   A. People

   B. Spiritual

   C. Financial
      1. What are trends, endowments, and so forth?

   D. Facilities

   E. Equipment

IV. Assumptions — List at least four

V. Functional Analysis

   A. Financial Analysis
      1. Analyze current financial situation
         a. Financial statements
      2. What tools would be beneficial in analysis?
         a. Pro forma statements for profit centers such as a bookstore
         b. Cash budget
         c. Capital budget
         d. Ratio analysis
         e. Operating and/or financial leverage
         f. Time value of money
         g. Break-even/C.V.P.
         h. Rate of returns
      3. Analysis of current financial policies
         a. Cash policies
         b. Accounts receivable
            (1) Discounts
            (2) Aging schedules
            (3) Collections

    c. Accounts payable
      (1) Discounts
    d. Inventory levels
    e. Debt retirement
  4. Synopsis of current financial situation

B. Accounting analysis

  1. Analysis of current accounting policies
    a. Depreciation
    b. Tax considerations
    c. Decentralized/centralized operations
    d. Responsibility accounting
  2. Tools beneficial in analysis
    a. Budgeting (short- and long-range)
    b. Variance analysis
    c. Break-even/C.V.P.
    d. Costing methods
    e. Contribution margin analysis
  3. Synopsis of current accounting situation
  4. Are these adequate controls, especially of cash at Sunday services?

C. Market analysis

  1. Analysis of current marketing policies
    a. Consumer
    b. Competition
    c. Product (type of product, type of demand, market position)
    d. Distribution channels (place, middleman, and so forth)
    e. Pricing (markups, discounts, commissions, contributions, and so forth)

      f. Promotion (advertising, selling, budget policies)

  2. Synopsis of current market situation

D. Management analysis

  1. Plan — Do you have a planning system? How does it work?

  2. Organize — Is organization of resources correct? (Show present organizational chart.)

  3. Direct — Centralized or decentralized?

  4. Staff — What needs do they have for people?

  5. Control — Are controls in evidence? What are they?

  6. Is there a motivation problem?

  7. Is strategy defined? What is strategy now?

  8. Synopsis of management situation

  9. How efficient is production function?

  10. Synopsis of Current Marketing/Public Relations Situation

VI. Computer Systems

  A. Determine need for a computer system

  B. What areas need to be analyzed?
    1. Church membership
    2. Church mailings
    3. Financial systems
    4. Information systems
    5. Inventory control
    6. Networking

VII. Legal analysis — Know law affecting churches.

VIII. Objectives

    A. Are they in key result areas?

    B. Are the objectives specific, measurable, and for a set time frame?

    C. Are there long- and short-term objectives?

IX. Strategies — List several for each key result area

X. Other

    A. Insurance, buildings, automobile liability, and so forth. This stage in the planning process is not just gathering data, getting it on paper, and forgetting about it. The environment must be constantly monitored. (It is like when I fish with Pastor Charles Farah. We have a strategy and enjoy our fishing and discussions. We are watching the clouds, wind and weather. If we see a front coming through and clouds rolling in we change our plan in a hurry. The same thing holds for church planning. Watch what is going on and be prepared to change.)

NOW LIST KEY ENVIRONMENTAL FACTORS FOR YOUR PLAN

NATIONAL:

REGIONAL:

LOCAL:

ASSESSING STRENGTHS AND WEAKNESSES

4

Assessing Strengths and Weaknesses

After we have identified our purpose and considered the environment in which we operate, we must assess the strengths and weaknesses of our church. Planners need to learn from athletic coaches in this area. They are constantly assessing the strengths and weaknesses of their team and the opponent. They try to maximize their strengths on game day, and during practice improve on their weaknesses. Howard H. Stevenson states:

> Business organizations have certain characteristics — strengths — which make them uniquely adapted to carry out their tasks. Conversely, they have other features — weaknesses — which inhibit their abilities to fulfill their purposes. Managers who hope to accomplish their tasks are forced to evaluate the strengths and weaknesses of the organization . . . (47).

Some of the things to consider might be your basic resources: human, financial, facilities, equipment, natural resources. White suggests:

1. Financial resources of the church including operating funds, special funds, income, and expenditures

— What has been our performance over the last five years in adhering to budget limits?

— What is our ability to raise funds when needed?

2. Equipment and space

— Is it adequate for present needs and for planning future needs?

— Is it in good operating condition?

— Is it costly to maintain or operate?

3. The demographics of our congregation

— How many people do we have in each age group?

— What are the basic categories of jobs and income levels?

— What percentage of the congregation consists of retired people or widows?

4. Sociological profile of our church

— Are we conservative or liberal?

— Are we community minded?

— Does our church collaborate with other community agencies and institutions?

— As a church, what are our primary interests and social values?

5. Power structure of the church

— Who makes the decisions and by what process?

6. Church organization and management

— Quality of staffing, lay leadership, personnel policies, financial, and business management capabilities, organizational structure.

7. Present programs
   — What are they?
   — Is the leadership in each program effective?
   — How much interest and support from the congregation does each program have?

It is fairly easy to identify the strengths in each. When you attempt to define weaknesses, it becomes a little more painful. Often, organizations must call in outside consultants to be able to candidly pinpoint their limitations. *But weaknesses and limitations must be recognized before you move on.* All the analyses listed in the environmental analysis can be separated into strengths and weaknesses.

I often have church planning groups identify strengths first and write them on a blackboard. Through discussions, the group agrees on perhaps five major strengths. I then have persons write two or three weaknesses of the organization down on paper, which I copy onto the board to generate discussion. Only with a realistic appraisal of strengths and weaknesses can realistic objectives be set.

"...founding pastors' [good health] is important to the continued success of their ministries."

5

Making Assumptions

The next stage is to make your major assumptions. These should be made about spheres over which you have little or absolutely no control; e.g., the external environment. One good place to start is to extend some of the items studied in the Environmental Analysis. Should this stage appear relatively unimportant in developing a long-range plan, consider this:

1. If you assume there will be no labor strikes in the upcoming year, the average inventory objectives might be lower than if you assumed there would be a strike.

2. More than likely all the automotive companies have assumed that no oil embargo will be imposed next year. Consider how their plans and objectives would change if they assumed an embargo loomed in the offing.

3. Not long ago, any church or ministry along the Texas Coast might have assumed that the Navy port being considered would be (or not be) in their area. Some assumptions could be made on location of a new General Motors plant being considered for one of twenty states.

Other business assumptions might relate to:

1. Trends in the stock market

2. Health of key managers

3. Adequate supply of key raw materials

4. Governmental regulation climate.

This stage is elementary, and it will help you identify all the important factors you feel will remain constant. (If any one changes drastically, major revisions in plans might be needed.)

Assumptions inherent in the field of church management might well include:

1. Television and radio programming costs will continue to skyrocket, especially during "prime time."

2. Church-related capital will remain tax exempt, and contributions to church organizations will continue to be tax deductible.

3. Nursery care during the Sunday morning service will remain a priority item sought after by mothers of infants.

4. Providing for a "family night" service during the week will continue to (a) enhance church unity and (b) be an effective means to teach members on such issues as proper tithing practice.

A common thread is noted in church ministries that are growing and thriving under their founders. At both Victory Christian Center of Tulsa and Calvary Temple of Tampa plans have the basic assumption that Billy Joe Daugherty and Dale Brooks remain in good health and remain as senior pastors. These founding pastors are important to the continued success of their ministries.

A denominational church will not have as big an immediate problem in the area of pastor replacement. If Dr. James Buskirk of Tulsa's First United Methodist were to leave, as well loved and popular as he is, that church could take his replacement in stride easier than Victory or Calvary could replace its pastor.

Defining Church Assumptions

Doug Murren, pastor of Eastside Foursquare Church in Kirkland, Washington, has listed certain assumptions that characterize his church. Assumptions, according to Murren, are those thoughts and ideas that we take for granted about ourselves, God, and others. These assumptions are basic beginning points in the church's care, interest and concern for people. Murren believes that if his people assume certain basics when they minister, the work of Christ will always be accelerated and accentuated in their lives and the life of their church.

My definition of *assumption* is "something over which you have little or no control." Here are some of his twenty-one assumptions that fit my planning model:

Quality leads to quantity. The quality of faith leads to greatness of faith. The quality of care for people leads to more people. (Note: Eastside Church places great emphasis on pastoral care, believing this is the best means of evangelism. A commitment to excellence produces confidence in ministry and in care. If I am committed to excellence in my personal life spiritually, emotionally, educationally, professionally, and socially, then people will have confidence in my interest in and care of them. The Holy Spirit, along with the church, is able, willing, and free to break in and carry on His work in non-spectacular, non-manipulative and surprising ways. Each church is a new creation and should have differing forms of style and practices suited to that particular group. You cannot manufacture the Holy Spirit's genuine working. You can only be in a position to see and enjoy it when it happens. Most of ministry involves focus, pinpointing and ridding ourselves of distractions. These factors can be considered when developing the assumptions on which the plan is based. (Note the following discussion of how the environmental analysis stage interacts with the assumption stage.)

Environmental Analysis:

1. Navy looks for homeport for battleship fleet.

   Location is possible in any state along Gulf Coast.

   Will generate $50 million payroll.

   $100 million in construction.

   3,000 civilian jobs.

   "Navy panel wraps up study of Houston as Homeport," *The Sun/The Daily Herald,* Saturday, March 23, 1985.

Assumption:

1. Assume that battleship fleet port will be located in Lake Charles, Louisiana, area.

The plan for a church in the Lake Charles, Louisiana, area is based in part on the environmental analysis that has thoroughly looked at what is going on in that area. In this case, you see that there is a chance for real economic change, new prosperity, people moving in, and so forth. Then you base your plan on an assumption. You either assume the port is in your area or you do not. How does this translate into action?

Analysis:

That overgrown lot next to the church that has been an eyesore for years will go up in value in a hurry if the port is located in the area. Now is the time to negotiate an option to buy to cover a two-year period, not in five years when the need is great and the price is sky high. The planner should also protect the church if the naval base goes somewhere else. With declining industry in the area, it is possible land values could go down.

The key is knowing what is going on and being alert to opportunities. Then develop a full plan based on a few assumptions. If an assumption changes, the plan changes.

LIST THE ASSUMPTIONS ON WHICH YOUR PLAN IS BASED

"...An archer that just shoots off anywhere
is liable to hit almost anything..."

6

Objectives, Targets, and Goals

Often I use the words *key results, goals* and *targets* synonymously with objectives. When thinking about both long- and short-term objectives, think of an archer drawing an arrow and aiming at a target. The bulls-eye represents exactly where you want to be at a certain point in time. A pastor wants his whole church aimed at the same target just as an archer wants his arrow aimed at the target. At the other extreme, an archer that shoots his arrows off in any direction is liable to hit almost anything — including the wrong target. People get confused and disorganized if they do not know where they are going.

Management by objectives has caused a stir in all areas of organizational life over the past twenty years. We need to remember that the word *management* is the key, or *the use of objectives to help manage for results*. We used my definition of SLRP/MBO at Oral Roberts University in the Business School during my tenure as dean from 1975-1986, and it proved very effective in developing a results-oriented, dynamic business school.

Before discussing the process of writing objectives, we must again refer to this new definition of SLRP/MBO presented earlier in this book. The purpose of the unit (ministry or church) must be defined, environmental analysis looked at, strengths and weaknesses assessed, and assumptions made. Then, and only then, can objectives be considered.

Sub-unit objectives must be clear, concise, written statements outlining what is to be accomplished in a key priority area, in a certain time period, in measurable terms that are consistent with the overall objectives of the organization. Objectives can be classified as routine, problem solving, innovative, team, personal, and budget performance. Drucker holds that "objectives are not fate; they are direction. They are not commands, but they *are* commitment. They do not determine the future, but they *are* the means by which the resources and energies of the operation can be mobilized for the making of the future" (8, p. 102). Objectives can be set at upper organizational levels in:

1) Profitability and growth, 2) market position and penetration, 3) productivity, 4) product leadership, 5) employee morale, development and attitudes, 6) physical and financial resources, 7) public responsibility (12, p. 117).

Every church administrator should use this outline as a basis for setting objectives for the church. Five-year objectives can be set in areas such as attendance, programs offered by the church, missionary support, building programs, and so forth. My good friend, Dale D. McConkey, in his book *Goal Setting; A Guide to Achieving the Church's Mission*, suggests objectives in Step 2:

Select "Key Result Areas" which are:

1. Level of membership

2. Level and sources of funds

3. Neighborhood acceptance

4. Youth participation

5. Quantity of programs

6. Quality of programs

7. Leadership effectiveness

8. Quantity and quality of services. (26, p. 21)

An article entitled "Charities Need a Bottom Line Too," published in the *Harvard Business Review,* covers six reasons why nonprofit organizations fail to set clearcut goals:

1. Many nonprofit managers fear accountability

2. Many projects continue even when they no longer serve an organization's goals

3. Nonprofits normally undertake any activity for which money is available

4. Some nonprofit managers fear hard-nosed evaluation may undermine humanitarian instincts

5. Nonprofit managers must spend a great deal of time on activities that do not further their goals (meeting with donors, fundraising, explaining programs, and so forth)

6. Nonprofits have no financial report cards to tell them how they are doing. (16, pp. 14-22)

The success or failure of a nonprofit organization is based on its ability to set goals, as well as on tools with which to measure progress. I agree with the six reasons for failure to set goals listed above. Also, a budget for five-year (long-range) programs must be developed. As objectives are set down into the organization, some of those mentioned above are not applicable. However, I believe this list could be applied in any type of organizational setting.

ORU First Lady Evelyn Roberts has said, "You cannot achieve goals if you do not have any. Sometimes this idea is so simple that many people overlook it. In order to accomplish anything, we have to first purpose in our hearts to do it. We have to make up our minds. If we do not, we just waste our time and energy and find ourselves going around in circles, looking back at the past and wondering where it went" (40, pp. 10, 11).

Performance Contract

As an example, note how the objectives for an associate pastor can become a performance contract through the following process:

1. Properly written objectives submitted to the pastor

2. Items discussed and negotiated with the pastor

3. Resubmitted to the pastor

4. List approved by both parties (and perhaps the pastor/parish relations committee).

5. In some organizations, both parties sign an objectives sheet.

Periodic Review

One practical, easy way to record, communicate, measure, and update objectives is through a "Performance Plan Book" or "Management Plan Book." All objectives for the organization should be in this book. Objectives are to be reviewed each quarter and updated. Following are examples of how objectives can be listed, kept track of, and presented for review. This process greatly reduces paperwork and provides a convenient method for review. Examples are of overall church objectives that encourage a looking to the future. They take into account key result areas and suggestions by more than fifty pastors and scholars.

OBJECTIVES

	1988	1989	1990
STAFF			
Pastor			
Assistants			
ATTENDANCE			
First Services	400	600	700
Second Services	500	600	700
Sunday School	400	500	600
Sunday Night	300	300	600
Wednesday Night	200	300	600
Revivals			
Training Seminars			
MEMBERSHIP	1500	2000	2200
BUILD A NEW CHURCH	Raise $500,000	Start 6/1/86	Complete 9/1/88
Facilities Improvements			
Added Equipment			
MISSIONS OUTREACH			
Contribution (to Central Fund)	$29,000	$30,000	$39,000
Other Mission Trips			
Annual Mexico Trips	2	3	4

OBJECTIVES

	1988	1989	1990

MISSIONS OUTREACH (Continued)

    Calling (Lay) People Involved

    Number of Calls

    1. Evangelism

    2. Hospital

    3. Posthospital

    4. NEO inactives

    5. Inactives

    6. Home department

    7. Nursing homes

FACILITIES

    Annual safety check

    Sound system

    Heating and cooling

    Burglar alarms

    Lighting

    Parking

PROGRAMS

    Children, Youth,

    Young adults, College age

    Men, Women, Senior citizens

    Divorce recovery

    Widowed

    Alcoholic recovery

    Marriage enrichment

    Caring calling

    Family life

OBJECTIVES

	1988	1989	1990

PROGRAMS (Continued)

    Political and social action

    Lay ministry training

PEOPLE/TRAINING/MORALE

	1988	1989	1990
House training per staff		20	2020
Retreat days for minister		5	710

    Retreat days for laity

    Retreats

    Yearly attitude survey

    Small groups: types, number, participants

    Counseling

    Ministerial

    Lay

    Alcoholics, Drugs

    Divorcees/Widows

PUBLIC RESPONSIBILITY

    Use facilities for Rotary lunches

    Sponsor Boy Scout and Girl Scout Troop

    Social Service

    Relief

    Talking books

    Prison ministry

    Meals on wheels

    Personal growth

        1. Initiate daily devotions

        2. Attend Growth Seminars

FINANCIAL

	1988	1989	1990
Average collections (per service)	$7,000	$8,000	$10,000

OBJECTIVES

	1988	1989	1990
FINANCIAL (Continued)			
Budget	$600,000	$800,000	$1,000,000
Current ratio	2/1	2/1	2/1
New tithers			
New pledgers			
Stewardship of persons			
New persons accepting responsibility			
New lay ministers			
New candidates for ordained ministry			
Fixed Asset Turnover/Collections/Net Fixed Assets			
Total Asset Turnover/Collections/Total Assets			
Debit Ratio/Total Debt/Total Assets			
Debt/Total Collections			
Times Interest Earned/Collections/Interest			

1989 MANAGEMENT PLAN

OUR OBJECTIVES	3-1-89	7-0-89	9-0-89	12-1-89

I. Routine
    Set aside $5,000 for
    overseas missions
    programs throughout
    every month of 1989   On target

II. Problem Solving
    Develop an efficient
    transportation routing
    schedule to be followed
    by the bus outreach
    captains by March 31,
    1989   Met 90%

III. Innovative
     Devise a better layout for
     member parking during
     February 1989.   Done

IV. Personal
    Read the book, *MBO:*
    Blue Collar to Top
    Executive, attend ORU
    Communication Course,
    fall of 1989.

V. Budget Performance
    Operate within the
    $50,000 fiscal church
    budget throughout 1989   On target

Lambert's book, *Managing Church Groups* (21, pp. 5-13), has helpful suggestions for writing objectives. Some fit into what I am trying to emphasize. Others are not covered in this chapter. He says:

1. Objectives should start with the word *to* followed by an action verb, since the achievement of an objective must come as a result of specific action.

2. Objectives should specify a single major result to be accomplished so the group will know precisely when the objective has been achieved.

3. An objective should have a target date for accomplishment.

4. The objective should relate directly to the mission statement of the group or individual. A parish council liturgy committee should not write an objective outside the scope of its own mission statement or one that pertains more to the mission statement of the parish council. This may seem obvious, but groups often commit themselves to projects for which they have neither responsibility nor authority.

5. The objective must be understandable to those who will be working to achieve the specified results.

6. It must be possible to achieve.

7. It should be consistent with parish and diocesan policies and practices.

Another example of a pastor's list of possible short-term objectives designed to support the overall church strategic plan is on the following page. Lambert's suggestions have been followed in making up this list.

CHURCH ADMINISTRATION OBJECTIVES

OUR OBJECTIVES   4-1-89   7-1-89   10-1-89   12-3-89

I.   *Routine Objectives*
1. To make at least one hospital visit per week in 1989
2. To exercise four times per week
3. To review each committee chairman's objectives and accomplishments by January 5, May 5, and August 5
4. To attend the annual state pastors' meeting.

II. *Problem-Solving Objectives*

1. To develop a project for the 11- to 14-year-old youth to make a contribution to the community by December 1989
2. To develop youth minister internship plan with local pastors by January 1989
3. To develop a set of criteria and measurable objectives for the Sunday School retreat by October 1989
4. To hold a one-day symposium on the spiritual and mental health of young people; to prepare summary minutes and recommendations for improvement by November 1989

III. *Innovative Objectives*

1. To devise a better system of screening prospective church employees by December 1, 1989
2. To develop a method or methods to give all committee chairmen feedback on their budget performance. At least one method to be implemented by May 1, and another method implemented by June 1, 1989

IV. *Personal Objectives*

1. To improve my understanding of the Bible: (I will read three pages per day and attend at least one Bible-study group during 1989.)
2. To not miss one Sunday service in 1989.

CHURCH ADMINISTRATION OBJECTIVES

OUR OBJECTIVES	4-1-89	7-1-89	10-1-89	12-3-89

V. *Team Objectives*

　　1. To work with the organist on revision and update of hymnbook to be introduced in July

　　2. To meet with the pastor each Wednesday to coordinate the music with the sermon

VI. *Budget Objectives*

　　1. To operate within the $100,000 yearly budget during 1989

　　2. To retire 10 percent of the debt on the church building in 1989

(Notice in Chapter 8 two actual examples from Calvary Temple International Christian Center under the leadership of Pastor Dale Brooks. The examples show how the Children's Ministry and Home Group Ministries have plans that support the overall strategic plan. Every church sub-unit must have specific detailed plans.)

"...Examples of strategy employed by church management could be:

UPGRADE MUSIC PROGRAM..."

7
Strategy

After objectives and goals have been set, a strategy must be developed to achieve them. Every objective must have a few key strategies. A good way to determine a strategy is to ask yourself: How and where am I going to commit my resources? Your answer will be your strategy. Or you might describe strategy as your "game plan." A basketball coach could use a strategy of shifting from a man-to-man defense to a zone press. It is during the strategy phase that we consider organizational structure.

Drucker says, "The best structure will not guarantee results and performances. But the wrong structure is a guarantee of nonperformance" (7).

During the strategy phase the organizational structure decision is made. In a new church program, strategy may/should include timing. (An example of strategy in real estate would be the decision whether or not to expand from residential units into industrial property.) Examples of such strategy would be: (1) determination of the amount and type of advertising, (2) horizontal or vertical integration, (3) level of research and development expenditures, and so forth. Strategy is the "thinking" stage of the long-range plan.

Examples of strategy employed by church management could be as follows:

1. Annex another section of land next to the church for more efficient parking.

2. Establish a trust to ensure funds are allocated toward the mission program.

3. Departmentalize the church budget in order that controls may be established to monitor the entire budgeting process.

4. Upgrade the music programs.

5. Introduce new programs in the fall.

6. A large downtown church could build a multilevel parking garage. During the week it could serve as a revenue generator and on the weekend handle congregations.

7. Time fund-raising appeals.

All strategies do not necessarily work as planned. For example, Bishop Emerson Colaw of the United Methodist Church said:

> Even the Methodist insistence on better education for its clergy has backfired. We have insisted our ministers be seminary-educated. They have acquired, along with that education, a taste for living in urban areas where museums, symphony orchestras, excellent libraries, and similar amenities are accepted as a way of life. No matter how many degrees a man has, if he is not prepared to love and serve the people and area where he is located, he is not equipped to conduct a successful ministry" (35, p. 9).

A team of ORU MBAs, under the direction of ORU faculty members Robert E. Stevens (now at Northeast

Louisiana University) and David Dyson, assisted *Christ Is The Answer,* located in El Paso, Texas, in developing a strategic plan. The communication strategy involved the use of various media to provide information, purpose, people, plans and programs. The communication strategy involved three key elements: *informing, persuading,* and *reminding.*

1. Informing

   This involves providing information to individuals and groups about the organizations. Specific elements of this plan call for:

   a. Use of video cassette presentations

   b. Newsletters, pamphlets, and prayer guides

   c. Personal speaking appearances by ministry leaders

   d. Hosting luncheons/dinners sponsored by supporters

   e. On-site visits by individuals/groups to headquarters or ministry centers.

2. Persuading

   This involves presenting the gospel message contained in the Great Commission as well as the principles from the apostle Paul's writings about the support he received while involved in mission work.

   a. Prepare application forms with which partners may request additional information or may apply as a team member.

   b. Provide opportunities for support by individuals through prayers and specific offerings for teams, supplies, and so forth.

3. Reminding

This aspect of the strategy is to continue to provide information to people already familiar with the ministry so they will be constantly reminded of the work and needs of the ministry.

a. Send letters/newsletters and other materials regularly.

b. Provide opportunities for team members to write supporters and future team members on a periodic basis.

c. Develop a complete file of individuals and organizations by name for future mailings.

I borrowed this exercise from a Boston consulting group and George Odiorne, who explained it on a napkin over breakfast one morning. You can evaluate almost anything with this matrix. One (1) is low and ten (10) is high. You can evaluate machines, people or programs. For example, on a planning retreat a church staff might make the following evaluations: choir (9,1); youth ministry (6,6); church library (8,8); newsletter (1,3); service attendance — 9:00 a.m. (9,3); 11:00 a.m. (9,7), and so forth.; and yearly potluck fundraiser (4,9). Each person should evaluate separately and then through discussion and negotiation arrive at final evaluations. Then you "polish stars," "solve problems," feed the "cows," and shoot "dogs."

High 10		
	CASH COWS (4,9) Fund Raiser	STARS Library (8,8) 11 a.m. (9,7) Youth (6,6)
P E R F O R M A N C E	DOGS (1,3) Newsletter	PROBLEM CHILDREN 9 a.m. (9,3) Chair (9,11)

Low 1 POTENTIAL **High 10**

This analysis helps make good strategic decisions. With limited resources, duplication, and so forth, each church or ministry must do a good job at important things and not dissipate resources so that little really gets done and in some cases causes the decline of the whole.

NOW DEVELOP MAJOR STRATEGIES TO MEET EACH OF THE OBJECTIVES

"...This is the 'action' or 'doing' stage..."

8

Operational Plans

After all the steps have been taken and a strategy has been developed to meet our objectives and goals, it is time to develop both a long- and short-range plan. Examples of where long-range plans should be made are in building for future expansion, equipment acquisition, and hiring to meet organizational needs, all of which are needed to obtain the desired results agreed upon in the stated objectives.

For example, Victory Christian Center has an energetic building plan to support its growth. The first phase will be approximately 120,000 square feet. When it was time to put the plan into action, Senior Pastor Billy Joe Daugherty announced that $5.77 million was needed in 1987-1988 for the building project. I salute Pastor Daugherty and his staff. They planned first and made building plans fit overall ministry plans. Too many times I have seen people build first and figure out what to do second. I predict a powerful ministry by this group in the year 2000.

It is important not to confuse objectives and strategy. This is the "action" or "doing" stage. Here you hire, fire, build, advertise, and so on. (Note Appendix C for a suggested method of keeping track of who is doing what on a short-term basis.) I have used this format for years. It works in business, in the church, and in your personal life. How many times has a group of people planned something, gotten enthusiastic and nothing happened? (Note the next several pages to see how to use the "Action Plan" format. Both are examples from the Calvary Temple plan.)

I have used Mark Opliger of Opliger Communications (39) in a wide range of work with ministries and churches. He has developed what he calls *COMMUNIQUE*. Each member of the staff fills out a short questionnaire which is then run through his computer. The result is a profile of each person's dominance, extroversion, patience, conformity, stress, and energy level. The profile helps each person understand his or her own behavior patterns. I use the profiles in a team-building exercise. Each person shares his profile with the group. Everyone understands each other better. It is especially important for everyone to understand the behavior patterns of the senior ministry or ministry leader.

During my years as dean of ORU's business school, the school's faculty filled out the questionnaire before an annual three-day planning retreat. We would then look at our profiles and be further reminded of our basic behavior traits. It helped us understand each other and work together better. I have used the *COMMUNIQUE* at *Back to the Bible Broadcast*, World Evangelism, portions of Oral Roberts' ministry, Calvary Temple, Victory Christian Center, First United Methodist Church, and the First Presbyterian Church.

Calvary Temple
ACTION PLAN
Home Groups

OBJECTIVE:

> To have 150 home groups in the next five years
>> 1991-1992: 135 to 150 home groups
>> 1990-1991: 90 to 95 home groups
>> 1989-1990: 62 home groups
>> 1988-1989: 45 home groups
>> 1987-1988: 30 home groups
>> 1986-1987: 20 home groups

STRATEGIES:

A. We plan to increase year by year as the total congregation grows so that we will be able to accommodate one-third to one-half of the congregation.

B. We plan to add one home group pastor for every fifty home groups.

ACTION PLAN	PERSON RESPONSIBLE	START DATE	DATE COMPLETED
Pastor Brooks is training several hand-picked couples as future home-group leaders.			
Each present home-group leader is in the process of training an assistant leader.			
Each existing home group, plus all new home groups are to set a goal to split and become two groups each year. They are to begin training an assistant within their new home group.			

Calvary Temple
ACTION PLAN
Children's Ministry

OBJECTIVE:

To have 500 children attending full children's church services during each of two adult morning services:

1991 — 500

1990 — 400

1989 — 450

1988 — 400

1987 — 300

STRATEGIES:

A. Develop complete teacher-recruitment training program

B. Develop neighborhood outreach ministry to children

C. Develop teacher training program

D. Develop puppet ministry

E. Hire full-time children's pastor.

ACTION PLAN	PERSON RESPONSIBLE	START DATE	DATE COMPLETED
Hire part-time pastor		1986	
Establish teacher-training course and teacher-recruitment strategy		1986	
Begin Saturday advertising campaign in community		1987	
Conduct four picnic-type outings year to attract local children		1987	
Full-time children's pastor hired		1988	
Puppet ministry		1988	
600 in two services		1989	
Update training services		1989	

Notice that the Action Plan format takes one objective out of the five-year strategic plan and isolates it for further study and analysis. In this case it shows the targets Calvary Temple is aiming toward with its Children's Ministry and Home Groups. You never go into action until the target is clear and understood by everyone. It is important that all those who execute these plans be in on the planning and be aware of what is going on. That is the key to enthusiasm and support by the people. With targets/objectives/goals in mind, the various strategies are agreed upon. They are listed right there under the objectives. Next, all the "actions" that must take place must be listed.

The person or persons responsible and the expected date of completion must be agreed upon. Every person involved gets a copy of the plan with his areas of responsibility marked. Now one person can coordinate a multitude of projects and programs, because there is a clear record of what is to be done. As each action or task is completed, the person responsible sends in a completion report. The coordinator knows what is going on all the time.

Periodic updates of the action plan are carried out so that everyone sees the progress. After people get accustomed to using the Action Plan format, they can discipline themselves. They do not want others to see they are falling behind. This is one of the greatest time saving, coordination ideas I have come up with in twenty-five years of professional work. We used it successfully in getting the ORU Women's Club cookbook published during my wife Mari's tenure as president. Can you imagine the complexity of dealing with more than 200 members, publishers, printers, and so forth? The Strategic Planning concept and the Action Plan worked like a charm. The ORU Women's Club cookbook has made enough money to contribute $29,000 to ORU women's scholarships. It was done as a 100 percent volunteer effort.

It is during this stage that the budget is prepared. The budget is the means to execute the plan. If the financial means to support the plan are not available, you must adjust the objectives. There is a constant interplay between the budget and the plan. Most people in America do not understand the budgetary process.

The budget is a "tool." Too often, however, the budget becomes the tail wagging the dog (or the church):

"We budgeted it so we had better spend it," and "We had better add a little to this year's budget" are statements that reflect this misunderstanding. Budgeted money must be tied directly to performance. Performance is measured against objectives. Key results and objectives in a church and ministry are prioritized. Money and resources are then allocated. An example of this interplay came out of a meeting at Calvary. Most of their resources for the next two years will go into finishing current building programs. Only enough money to maintain the status quo with the school is allocated. That does not mean the school is not important — it is. But the timing for expansion and growth cannot come and does not make sense until 1988. A well-thought-out plan suggested by everyone succeeds. How many times do you see churches and ministries trying to do everything at once? The word "strategic" in the title of this book implies thinking, praying, and seeking order. All this can happen if an Action Plan coordinates and supports the overall plan.

"...Outside areas of interest...receive the major part
of the enthusiasm and the independent and
innovative work..."

9

Appraisal and Reevaluation

The last stage, then, is to appraise the church and each of its entities to determine if all objectives have been met:

— Have the measurable objectives and goals been accomplished?

— How far did actual performance miss the mark?

— Did the attainment of the objectives and goals support the overall purpose?

— Has the environment changed enough to change the objectives and goals?

— Have additional weaknesses been revealed that will influence changing the objectives of the organization?

— Have additional strengths been added or your position improved sufficiently to influence the changing of your objectives?

— Has the ministry provided its members with organizational rewards, both extrinsic and intrinsic?

— Is there a feedback system to help members satisfy their high-level needs?

Please note how my brand of Long-Range Planning/MBO is easily revised. Note the various objectives and the quarterly review. If there is a deviation, the problem is "red flagged" and given attention. For example, when I was dean, I reviewed the ORU School of Business objectives and results with my boss at the end of each semester. If there was a major problem that would inhibit goal attainment, I would let him know immediately.

Part of the appraisal process is the reward system. This is difficult to manage.

To determine if the organizational reward system is working properly, ask any member, "What is the most satisfying thing you do?"

If the respondent lists half a dozen items and his work is not included, you have an organizational problem. People are seeking satisfaction of the higher-level needs of self-esteem, recognition, and autonomy. If the church or ministry does not have the means of satisfying these needs, organizational members will go outside the organization to have these needs met. When this happens, the outside areas of interest — Girl Scouts, PTA, hobbies, and so on — receive the major part of the enthusiasm, and the independent and innovative work of the organization member. His job, and the organization itself, receive only base efforts. An organization can sustain itself for quite a while in such a situation. The loss is in the hard-to-measure factor of what could have been accomplished if every organization member was receiving at least some of his higher-level-need satisfaction from within the organization and was giving the resultant enthusiastic innovative support to the organization. All industries and organizations have a universal problem in giving extrinsic rewards for performance. Provision must be made for the person to satisfy higher-level needs *within* the organization. This can be done if MBO is used properly.

At the end of the performance year and as part of the thinking for the new year, the purpose, environment, strengths, weaknesses, and assumptions must be reevaluated.

Charles R. Wilson, in the series *Tools for Church Management,* covers twelve points and principles of performance evaluation. Six of his points that I view as the most important are:

1. Performance evaluation must be self-evaluation

4. Performance evaluation is for healthy, performing, growing individuals.

6. Evaluation is subjective

8. "No evaluation" is not an option

9. When an evaluation process is perceived as legitimate, fair, and working, people will tend to use it responsibly. When it is not, people will still do something . . . but they may not feel the burden of responsibility.

12. Performance evaluation is a formal process. (59)

It is in the appraisal stage that every church and ministry with whom I have worked really got hooked on the strategic concepts outlined in this book. Recent experiences include sitting in on a review of progress by Brian Erickson, executive director of *Back to the Bible Broadcast,* and Dale Brooks, pastor of Calvary Temple. For Erickson, it was routine after years of formal, well-done reviews and status reports. For Brooks, it was his first review. In both cases there was a sense of pride, accomplishment, and excitement by all concerned.

People at all levels need to know of the progress being made toward fulfilling the overall plan. Erickson had, just a few days earlier, reported plan progress to his governing board.

This brand of strategic planning won't work without a review of performance.

NOW LIST THE WAYS YOU CAN REWARD PEOPLE FOR ACHIEVING THEIR GOALS AND CONTRIBUTING TOWARD THE OVERALL PLAN:

NOW LIST THE THINGS THAT CAN BE DONE TO COACH AND ENCOURAGE THOSE WHO NEED IMPROVEMENT:

STRATEGIC LONG-RANGE PLAN
QUARTERLY REVIEW: 1986

CALVARY TEMPLE   1986
DEPARTMENT: Overall Ministry

OBJECTIVES	1ST QTR Jan-Mar	2ND QTR Apr-Jun	3RD QTR Jul-Sept	4TH QTR — Oct-Dec —	TOTAL 1986 Actual

A. Attendance
   1. Goal Per week: Adults   1050
                                          Youth   250
                                                  1300

B. Home Groups
   1. Number of groups: 20   18

C. Youth
   1. Attendance: 300   250
   2. Rock Groups: 16   13
   3. Percentage: 53%   45%

Reported by: _____ Date: /   /

Page: ___ of ___

"...purpose, environment, strengths, weaknesses and assumptions must be re-evaluated."

10

Conclusion

In conclusion, the question arises whether or not all this extensive planning and work are worth the effort. I have been actively pursuing the answer to this question since 1978. I now feel confident that the answer is an overwhelming yes. A number of pastors who attended the Pastor's Conference in Florida in 1984 have implemented this planning and management system based on the seminar sessions and the handouts at that meeting. I have a file of letters confirming the successes they feel they have achieved.

One ministry into which I put a lot of time and effort achieved dramatic results quickly. These results can be measured in many ways. One particular way is the effectiveness with which the ministry team planned and managed. I first introduced the "Management System Balance Sheet" concept in my book, *An MBO Approach to Long-Range Planning.* (31, p. 83) The Management System Balance Sheet is a tool partially borrowed from accounting. I worked out a way to take the asset and liability concept from accounting to determine the assets and liabilities in a ministry's planning and management system, based on the responses of people working in the ministry.

In a ministry where we started working with this concept in July 1979, assets were shown of +0.1 and total liabilities of −3.8, with an improvement factor needed of 3.7. After strategic long-range planning, MBO, and working together, the improvement factor rose to a management system surplus of +0.9 by January 1980, and by June 1980, to +1.9. (Note Table I in this chapter for more details.)

Table II shows the results of the *Back to the Bible Broadcast's* "Management System Balance Sheet" indexes. Ministry personnel were excited by the Strategic Planning/MBO concept from the beginning. They methodically took their time and did things right. You can see by the perception of the people how the Management System Balance Sheet Index improved from +2.56 in 1980 to +5.79 in July 1985, and to +6.86 in July 1986. One key factor in their success was their willingness to take the time to do things properly. With a long-term view, they dedicated a lot of time to improving their planning and management system. They even went to the extent of installing a performance appraisal and salary administration similar to what is outlined in Chapter 6 of my books, *An MBO Approach to Long-Range Planning* (31) and Strategic Long-Range Planning (29). They are one of the few ministries and churches that I know have tied the reward system into their strategic plan. I feel they are a model for many churches and ministries to follow.

From recent efforts with Victory Christian Center in Tulsa and Calvary in Tampa, Florida, I hear reports of many positive benefits and can see positive things happening in those ministries as well. Only time will tell if the two ministries remain successful. Obviously, there is more to success than doing a good job of planning and managing, but I do not think you can be successful without it.

I just received a letter from a frustrated and hurt pastor who said he tried all this, and the elders replaced him. He asked me to warn others to be careful, which I have. I feel there were other serious problems, and the planning effort only exposed these problems. However, I am in no position to judge that situation without knowing the circumstances. This philosophy of managing, planning, and organization is a tool that can be used to serve God. It is like an airplane. It, too, can serve God, but if used improperly, can crash.

Dr. Larry Lea, ORU's vice president of spiritual affairs and senior pastor of Church on the Rock in Dallas, has much to offer in the realm of planning and management as well as in spiritual teaching and in preaching. In his book, *Mending Broken Nets and Broken Fishermen*, he raises two very important issues: the possibility of planning becoming mechanical and of leaving God out of the plan (22, p. 119). In Chapter 8 of his book, Lea states his "Fundamental #5: The Restoration of Goal-Oriented Leadership":

> Many of God's fishermen alternate between the extremes of busy bustle or burnout; either tugging frantically at the oars to reach some man-made objective, or lying exhausted and disillusioned in the bottom of a drifting boat after the net has returned empty, torn and tangled again.

> The restoration of goal-oriented leadership is the answer. However, when I speak of restoring goal-oriented leadership, I am not referring to "hype," positive mental attitude or man-made and man-motivated

objectives; rather, I am referring to Spirit-imparted goals and Spirit-empowered fishermen.

The restoration of goal-oriented leadership is absolutely essential if God's church is to grow spiritually and numerically. But how are such goals initiated and implemented? What are the implications of goal-oriented leadership for the kingdom of God?

He continues in that chapter to make the following points:

1. When programs and projections take the place of prayer; when surveys and panel discussions take the place of prophetic insight; when scholarship takes the place of spiritual gifts, we are too sophisticated for the Holy Spirit.

2. Fellow fishermen, if we do not have goals, we will become stagnant.

3. Another spiritual danger encountered in goal-oriented leadership is imitation. We copy all the latest programs; we scan the opinion polls and surveys; we copy rather than create; we imitate rather than initiate. We succumb to the deadly cycle of comparing and competing.

4. How are goals initiated? Not by sophistication. Not by stagnation. Not by imitation. The fisherman's goals must be initiated by the Holy Spirit.

5. We must get down before God and ask, "Lord, what is Your will? What is Your goal?" We must let Him set the goal, because when He implants His goal in us, He also imparts the faith to see it fulfilled.

I interpret his book and this chapter to say, "do not leave God out of the plan."

We should use all the sophistication and experience contained in this book to gather and organize the plan. However, the plan must serve the vision. Openness to the Holy Spirit can confirm and direct the plan. Lea's management style also is interesting in that he is using a philosophy of management that Katz and Kahn proved in their studies at the University of Michigan years ago. (32) Pastor Lea hires exceptional people and leaves them alone. He also brings people of great ability and drive into his organization, even if there is not a specific slot in the organizational chart. This is somewhat contrary to what we study and learn in many of our business texts. Pastor Lea uses a very powerful principle: the proper managing and use of the best resource — people.

Contrast this with what I have seen in many ministries and churches. There is a tendency by many good people to want to sign every letter, dot every "i", and control the entire organization. This tendency cannot be faulted if good people in their spirits are trying to learn to do the right thing. However, there is a fault when a person in authority is not willing to learn proper planning and management characteristics. It has been proved and documented that all organizations go through four specific evolutionary stages. In each evolutionary stage, the method of planning, management, and control must change.

A mistake can be forgiven the first time, but I feel it should not be forgiven if it is repeated time and time again. Pastors and heads of ministries must learn to delegate, to help their people grow, and to give responsibility and accountability to the people working for them. There is an underlying element of trust. If a ministerial or church employee has to have approval for everything, that person is working under a spirit of fear, trying to avoid criticism, and in the process his or her own self-worth is destroyed.

I have worked with one major ministry that has had almost no management turnover in ten years. I know of another that has about 50 percent turnover every year.

Pastor Lea and his senior staff operate in a spirit of love. There is a constant loving, coaching, and affirming atmosphere that finds its way down through his organization. I have worked in churches and ministries where the spirit of fear was so great that you could cut it with a knife. Pastor Lea is giving us a model to work under in this area.

My good friend Sam Ventura of Dallas shared Lea's philosophy of managing with me.

He says, "It is the leader's responsibility to bring out the best in people. There is a difference between management and leadership. The key should be leading people, not managing people. A leader inspires, creates vision and loyalty, and that style creates a sense of excitement in the organization. Managing implies control and manipulation, which creates an employee who is not as happy on the job."

That is a powerful statement for all pastors to consider. It would be interesting if, at the end of each day, a pastor or person in authority in a church or ministry would ask:

"What did I do today to cause our people to grow?"

If he cannot list very many things, then it is possible he has exercised too much control and cast a shadow of fear. His employees may have gone home with feelings of frustration, guilt, and lack of self-worth. Look at the effect this could have on relationships at home, based on what happened at work that day.

Tables follow.

TABLE I

MINISTRY BEFORE LONG-RANGE PLANNING/MBO
Assets

	July 1979
Freedom to work	+0.1
Total assets	+0.1

Liabilities

Goals	-0.6
Planning	-0.5
Planning ineffectiveness	-0.2
Low morale	-0.6
Performance appraisal	-0.7
Performance reward	-0.6
Communication	-0.2
Job dissatisfaction	-0.4
Total liabilities	-3.8

Surplus

Improvement factor needed	-3.7

MINISTRY AFTER LONG-RANGE PLANNING/MBO
Assets

	January 1980	June 1980
Goals	+0.2	+0.0
Planning	+0.0	+0.0
Planning effectiveness	+0.4	+0.0
Performance appraisal	+0.0	+0.0
Performance reward	+0.2	+0.0
Freedom to supervise	+0.0	+0.6
Communication	+0.2	+0.1
Job satisfaction	+0.2	+0.1
Total assets	+1.2	+1.9

Liabilities

	January 1980	June 1980
Low morale	-0.3	-0.0
Total Liabilities	-0.3	-0.0

Surplus

	January 1980	June 1980
Management system surplus	+0.9	+1.9

Table II

Back to the Bible Broadcast
Using Strategic Planning/MBO

MANAGEMENT SYSTEM BALANCE SHEET

ASSETS	OCT 1980	FEB 1981	NOV 1981	DEC 1982	JULY 1985	JULY 1986	JULY 1987
Goals	+0.60	———	+0.59	+0.67	.89	.98	1.08
Planning	+0.27	+0.00	+0.52	+0.84	.71	.95	.92
Planning Effectiveness	+0.04	+0.17	+0.20	+0.50	.24	.42	−0.01
Morale	+0.23	+0.83	+0.11	+0.32	.53	.62	.94
Performance Appraisal	+0.00	+0.33	+0.12	+0.44	.76	.95	.78
Supervision Balance	+0.64	+0.67	+0.53	+0.59	.96	1.00	.85
Communication	+0.46	+0.36	+0.25	+0.64	.75	.82	.67
Job Satisfaction	+0.37	+0.48	+0.55	+0.63	.79	.88	.33
Goals	———	−0.43					
Performance Reward System	−0.05	−0.41	−0.16	+0.34	+.16	+.34	.33
TOTAL ABILITIES MINUS TOTAL LIABILITIES	+2.56	+2.00	+2.71	+4.97	+5.79	+6.96	+5.89

TABLE III
Back to the Bible Broadcast
MANAGEMENT SYSTEM BALANCE SHEET

August 1986

ASSETS	TOTAL	DIRECTOR	SUPERVISOR	MANAGER
Goals	0.98	1.08	1.15	1.13
Planning	0.95	1.17	0.91	0.93
Planning Effectiveness	0.42	0.79	0.33	0.40
Morale	0.62	0.75	0.75	0.41
Performance Appraisal	0.95	1.08	1.06	0.78
Supervision Balance	1.00	1.30	1.07	0.85
Communication	0.82	1.00	0.80	0.77
Job Satisfaction	0.88	1.07	0.94	0.75
Performance Reward System	0.34	0.71	0.24	0.35
TOTAL ASSETS	6.96	8.95	7.25	6.37
LIABILITIES				

The best way to judge how a church or ministry is being managed is to look at the turnover rate at all levels. Most people want to contribute, work hard and be part of something great. God calls them to a place to make a contribution. In most cases they are competent. They leave a few years later discouraged, hurt, and depressed. I cannot count the times I have heard the statement "so-and-so did not catch the vision" and left. These leaders are misusing the Lord to overcome their lack of leadership abilities. The "God told me and you must obey" philosophy has run its course and is no longer acceptable.

Note the 1986 monthly budget for the Christ Is the Answer team in Mexico. This is an example of the accountability I believe a church and ministry needs to use.

Christ Is the Answer Mexico Team
Monthly Budget
1986

INCOME

Current Team Support	$2600.00	
	TOTAL	$2600.00

EXPENSES

Feeding Program	700.00
Permits/Utilities	385.00
Camp Supplies	375.00
Promotional Expense	335.00
Gasoline	240.00
Food	250.00
Vehicle Maintenance	350.00
Telephone	50.00
Postal & Administrative	50.00
TOTAL	2735.00

Operating Deficit   [$135.00]

MEXICO TEAM STATISTICS
- 40 Missionaries
- $50 per month expense, per missionary
- 375 people evangelized per missionary, per month
- 180,000 people evangelized per year
- Less than $.13 per person evangelized

The United Methodist Church uses many of the concepts outlined in this book. For example, they reported these objectives in *The United Methodist Reporter* (Sept. 26, 1986, p. 3):

1. A call to start at least 3,600 United Methodist congregations between 1988 and 2001 tops a list of long-range membership growth strategies being proposed to the Council of Bishops.

2. A total of $36 million is being sought, including $24 million the Board of Global Ministries plans to raise for church development. The other $8 million is to be raised within the 73 U.S. annual and missionary conferences for church planning in those areas.

3. Establish an annual membership goal each year in each congregation and report that goal to the bishop.

4. Capitalize on membership strength in the Sunbelt for future growth.

5. Increase worship attendance by 3 percent a year between 1988 and 2001. Organize a working evangelistic effort in each church every year.

6. Have a confirmation class in each church every year.

7. Establish 150 church schools each year in churches that do not have Christian education programs, or at satellite sites in a community.

8. Increase church school attendance by 3 percent a year.

9. Increase the number of youths involved in church programs by 10 percent each year.

10. Recruit 150 new directors or ministers of Christian education each year.

11. Double by 1992 the number of United Methodist students attending United Methodist-related colleges and participating in Wesley Foundation programs at state universities. Currently an estimated 25 percent of students at United Methodist colleges are United Methodists.

12. Identify 2,000 young people each year as candidates for ordained or diaconal ministry.

Based on the environmental factors:

1. Between 1966 and 1984, the denomination started 793 new churches.

2. The denomination closed some 300 churches each year during the same 18-year period. That equals a net loss of more than 4,000 churches.

Strategies to support objectives:

1. The committee is asking bishops to recruit 300 different churches each year to financially sponsor two new congregations someplace in the country.

2. The sponsorship concept allows church development funds to flow across annual conference borders.

3. To supplement funds raised by local "mother" churches, the committee is calling for various agencies within the denomination to set aside $3 million annually between 1988 and 2001 for new-church development.

4. Capitalize on membership strength in the Sunbelt for future growth.

This conclusion then should go into the Operational Plan for any United Methodist Church:

1. Church law makes each annual conference responsible within its own borders for starting and financing new local churches.

The First United Methodist Church of Tulsa, under the able leadership of Dr. James Buskirk and his staff, must consider these broad overall objectives, environmental factors, strategies, and plans as they develop their strategic long-range plan for First United Methodist here in Tulsa. Unlike nondenominational and ministry-dominated churches, denominations such as the United Methodists, Baptists, Presbyterians, and Catholics, to name a few, must be aware of the need to have their individual church plans support the overall denominational plans. It shows insight and accountability for the Methodist central leadership to establish these central objectives, goal targets and key result areas. It helps the local church, such as the First United Methodist in Tulsa, to better establish its niche, direction and plans.

Some of the obvious benefits of all this begin to show up almost immediately. The senior pastor has a strong, committed team. People all pull together in a united effort. They are no longer individuals concerned solely about their own areas. Coordination has improved because everyone knows what others are doing. Communication has improved in all directions. All the problems listed at the beginning of the first chapter begin to fade away. The senior pastor all of a sudden has time on his hands to do what he feels called to do. I have seen it happen repeatedly.

Care must be exercised, however, to be sure that a mistake made in industry is not duplicated in ministries and churches. In the Sixties, many got on the MBO bandwagon. In the Seventies, there was a rush toward strategic planning. Many of these efforts failed. In my experience and observation of these failures I saw many reasons, but there was always a common thread. The common problem was lack of understanding of the fundamentals. With MBO, many books had a little formula: set objectives, review, and sit back and watch performance improve. With strategic planning, it was "get a five-year plan, computerize it, and you will be home free." Nothing will work over the long term unless the following fundamentals are met:

1. Recognition that all people work to satisfy higher-level needs of personal growth, recognition, and opportunity for independent thought and action.

2. The plan must be in writing.

3. Those who execute the plan must be in on the planning.

4. There must be an open, trusting climate and culture in the organization.

5. Maintain the belief that people will work, be loyal.

6. Every department and functional area has a support plan with well-defined expected results.

7. Every person has a plan for his job, including well-defined expected results.

8. Progress on results versus the overall plan expectation should be openly reviewed four times per year and reported to everyone.

9. Constant feedback of information of all types is vital.

10. Encourage creativity, new ideas.

11. Each person has the opportunity no less than twice per year to review performance with his boss.

12. Develop a reward system to encourage the achievers and assist the average performers and nonperformers to improve.

13. A people plan must include development for everyone.

14. Develop a control system that includes a sensible budget.

Back to the Bible Broadcast has made strides in all fourteen of these areas. It is no surprise that they have high scores on the MSBS year after year. They view strategic planning and MBO as a top priority. They passed the critical fifth-year test.

I have found in business, industry, and nonprofit a tendency to get lazy in that fifth year. Things start running so smoothly that attention to the fourteen points starts to dwindle.

One major ministry that I served as a consultant got a plan and had everything working, including the early stages of performance appraisal. A new general manager and the fifth-year hex killed the system. We had gone out for a scheduled review and I was told:

"Dr. Migliore, you have done so much for us. We are too busy for the year-end review. Just enjoy yourself."

I protested and was promised that a review would come right after the first of the year. I kept calling back to check, and it was always "We will do it next month." One slip: no year-end review. No chance for those who worked hard all year to show what they had done. No feedback to employees who wanted to know what was going on. One slip leads to another. The next five-year plan is based on reviewing the past year, dropping that year, and extending the plan another year.

Now the organization was operating with no agreed-upon short-term plan. I kept saying, "Better get a plan," and was told "Too busy; we need to just wrap up a few problems." That day never came, and by midyear, confusion, and frustration reigned. One longtime employee told me, "We are back to square one." They are making an attempt to get strategic planning going.

In another big flop, I assisted a Christian university in developing a strategic plan for each of its schools. ORU MBAs on summer internships assisted and made a great contribution. Everything went fine until the end of the first semester. They never had even their first review. You guessed it — flop!

It is as simple as trying to make teenagers responsible and accountable for their chores. If you forget to review, reward, praise and suggest improvement, you might as well forget it.

In another major ministry no longer in existence, I was called in to assist. They were wonderful, warm, loving people. I was enjoying myself immensely as we progressed with our work. But I began to notice some inconsistencies. In the meetings it was "conquer" the world, triple in size — up, up, and away. In reality, facts were showing a declining partner base, and I would hear discussions about difficulty making the payroll. My planning sessions had, in reality, turned into cheerleading clinics while the ship was sinking. Top management would not confront the facts and face reality. As I pressed the issue to get down to brass tacks, I was lovingly thanked and not invited back. It was like a canoe heading for a waterfall, and no one wanted to shout, "Trouble ahead. We had better do something."

One pastor came to me defeated and in tears, "I started the church, it grew, we developed elders, and they just kicked me out."

It took less than sixty seconds for me to find the reason, and about three more hours for him to understand it. He had violated the basic fundamental of involving the people in the plan. The idea that "God talked to me, I have the plan, you follow me, and do what I say in the name of Jesus" just does not add up. It is more power than mortal man can handle. "God told me this, God told me that, you obey," can work for a while. But problems set in when things do not work out, and the seed of doubt creeps into people's minds.

This pastor realized that was his main problem. I prayed for him and he thanked me, feeling that at least he understood what had happened.

Another well-known TV evangelist openly says on nationwide television, "I do not plan, we do not plan,

God directs our steps. I wait each day for the Holy Spirit."

That means to me if God does not direct every step, they will tend to wander in circles and in confusion. The Bible says there should be order and no confusion. Powerful leaders with little accountability and control are slow learners. My prediction is that it will take a minimum of seven more years for this particular ministry to learn how to plan, manage, and operate properly. Heaven help the people working there who are confused, disillusioned, hurt, and suffering.

However, this book is not meant to be negative. These just-described situations are real, and we must learn from them. There is no attempt to embarrass anyone. If I wanted to be sensational and quadruple book sales, I would name names, times, and places. This book is written to serve His church, His ministry, His people.

As Lee Iaccoca says, "Success confirms what we know, and we learn from failure."

Anyone who has taken the time to read this far has been around and seen plenty of failures. Let us get all these failures, flops, and false starts out on the table and learn from them. Why repeat the same mistakes in your church or ministry?

My final suggestion is that you study what I have presented, pray about it, and ask others for advice. Keep in mind the fourteen key fundamentals, then go back to Chapter 1 and implement the planning process if you feel a confirmation from the Holy Spirit that you need to act on this information.

References

1. Arn, Win, "Understanding and Implementing Growth for Your Church."

2. Benjamin, D., Durkin, J., & Iverson, D., 1985. *The Master Builder* (Lake Tahoe: Christian Equippers International), pp. 27-55.

3. Boyce, L.F., ed. "Accounting for Churches," *Journal of Accountancy* (Feb. 1984), p. 96.

4. Buckingham, Jamie. *Ministries Today* (May-June, 1987), p. 23.

5. Buckingham, Jamie, 1982. "Having Visions — Dreaming Dreams," *Christian Leadership Letter*.

6. Ditzen, Lowell Russel, 1968. *The Minister's Desk Book* (New York: West Nyack, Parker Publishing Co., Inc.), p. 2.

7. Drucker, Peter, 1974. *Management: Tasks, Responsibilities, and Practices* (New York: Harper & Row), p. 79.

8. Drucker, Peter, 1954. *The Practice of Management* (New York: Harper), pp. 121-131.

9. Durkin, Jim. *The Master Builder*.

10. Fayol, H., 1949. *Industrial Administration* (London: Pitman).

11. Gladden, R. K., Green, N. M. Jr., & Rusbuldt, R. E., 1980. *Key Steps in Local Church Planning* (Valley Forge: Judson Press), pp. 11-81.

12. Gray, Gary, 1983. "Managing for the Future," *Church Management* (Aug.), pp. 10, 42.

13. Gray, R. N., 1971. *Managing the Church* (Enid: The Haymaker Press), Vol. 1

14. Gray, R. N. 1978. *Managing the Church: Business Administration* (Enid: The Haymaker Press), Vol. 2

15. Hale, Ashley. "Planning that Works," *Church Management* (Sept. 1984), p. 30.

16. Harvey, Phil & Sander, J., 1987. "Charities Need a Bottom Line, Too," *Harvard Business Review*, pp. 14-22.

17. Hendrix, O., 1976. *Management for the Christian Leader* (Milford: Mott Media), pp. 16, 35, 47-55.

18. Horvath, Jeff, 1987. *Study: Church Planning* (Tulsa: ORU Masters Thesis).

19. Humble, John. "Social Responsibility — The Contribution of MBO," *MBO Journal*, Vol. 5, No. 3, 19.

20. Hutcheson, R. G. Jr., 1979. *Wheel Within the Wheel* (Atlanta: John Knox Press).

21. Lambert, N. M., 1975. *Managing Church Groups* (Dayton: Pflaum Publishing).

22. Lea, Larry, 1985. *Mending Broken Nets & Broken Fishermen* (Rockwall: Church on the Rock), pp. 119-133.

23. Lindgren, A. J., 1965. *Foundations for Purposeful Church Administration* (Nashville: Abingdon Press), pp. 226-254.

24. Lindgren, A. J., 1977. *Management for Your Church* (Nashville: Abingdon Press), pp. 26, 34, 53, 60-66, 80, 140.

25. Maslow, Abraham, 1983. "A Theory of Human Motivation," *Psychological Review*, 50, 33-44.

26. McConkey, D. D., 1978. *Goal Setting: A Guide to Achieving the Church's Mission* (Minneapolis: Augsburg Publishing House), pp. 17-32.

27. McGavran, D., 1980. *Church Growth Strategies That Work* (Nashville: Abingdon Press), pp. 29,59.

28. McDonough, Reginald M., 1975. *Leading Your Church in Long-Range Planning* (Convention Press), p. 5.

29. Migliore, R. H., 1986. *Strategic Long-Range Planning* (Jenks: RHM & Associates).

30. Migliore, R. H., 1987. *Strategic Long-Range Planning in Churches and Ministries* (New York:).

31. Migliore, R. Henry, 1984. *An MBO Approach to Long-Range Planning* (Englewood Cliffs: Prentice Hall).

32. Migliore, R. Henry, 1974. *MBO: Blue Collar to Top Executive* (Washington, DC: BNA Press).

33. Migliore, R. Henry, 1986. *Develop a Strategic Plan for Your Life; A Biblical Perspective* (Dallas: WOF Press).

34. "Defining the Mission," *Christian Leadership Letter* (World Vision, June 1984), pp. 1,2.

35. Macklin, Beth. "Purpose, Goals Vital, Bishop Says of Methodist Church," *Tulsa World*, Sec. C, p. 9, February 20, 1985.

36. Mali, Paul, 1972. *Managing Objectives* (New York: Wiley).

37. Myers, F. Marvin, ed. "Trained Administrators Make a Difference," *Church Management* (March 1983), p. 34.

38. Odiorne, George, 1965. *Management by Objectives: A System of Managerial Leadership* (New York: Pitman Publishing Co.), p. 55.

39. Opliger, Mark, Opliger Communications, P. O. Box 78183, Wichita, Kansas 67278

40. Roberts, Evelyn. "How to Make 1977 the Most Exciting Year of Your Life," *Daily Blessing*, Vol. 19, No. 1 (1977), pp. 10-11.

41. Rusbuldt, Richard, 1980. *Key Steps in Local Church Planning.*

42. Schaller, L. E., 1965. *The Local Church Looks to the Future* (Nashville: Abingdon Press), pp. 33-, 46-670.

43. Schaller, L. E., 1971. *Parish Planning* (Nashville: Abingdon Press), pp. 102-117.

44. Schaller, L. E. & Tidwell, C. A., 1975. *Creative Church Management* (Nashville: Abingdon Press), pp. 55-65, 117-135, 192-203.

45. Schuller, Robert H. *Your Church Has a Fantastic Future.*

46. Shelley, M., 1985-86 Winter, "What's A Body To Do?" *Leadership.*

47. Stevenson, Howard H., Spring 1986. "Defining Corporate Strengths and Weaknesses," *Sloan Management Review*, pp. 52-67.

48. Strang, Stephen, Winter 1985-86, "Paul Younggi Cho Says Ministries Need Visions and Dreams," *Ministries Today*, pp. 44-46.

49. Tidwell, C. A., 1985. *Church Administration: Effective Leadership for Ministry* (Nashville: Broadman Press), pp. 58, 103-177.

50. Van Auken, Philip, and Johnson, Sharon G. *Church Administration* (May/June 1984), p. 85.

51. Wagner, C. P., 1986. *Church Growth: State of the Art* (Wheaton: Tyndale House Publishers), pp. 11, 15-39, 83-87.

52. Walrath, D. A., 1984. *Planning for Your Church* (Philadelphia: Westminister Press), pp. 37-95, 105.

53. Wesley, John, 1754. *Explanatory Notes Upon the New Testament*.

54. Wesley, John, 1743. *The Nature, Design and General Rules of the United Societies*.

55. Wesley, John, 1763. *Notes Upon the New Testament*.

56. Wesley, John, 1763. *Rules*.

57. Wesley, John, 1763. *Sermons*.

58. White, R. N., Peacock, P. R., Shively, R. W., & Ferner, J.D. *Managing Today's Church* (Valley Forge: Judson Press), pp. 25-39, 104-110, 131.

59. Wilson, Charles R. *Tools for Church Management*.

60. Wilson, Charles R. *Principles and Procedures in Performance Evaluation; Part I With the Performance Evaluation Kit* (Lebanon: CRW Management Service).

61. Wolf, William B., 1978. *Management and Consulting: An Introduction to James O. McKinsey* (New York: Cornell University Press).

62. Young, Randall, 1984. *A Study of Environment, Strategy, and Planning Processes in Churches* (The University of Mississippi).

Appendix A

Comments From Pastor's Workshops and Religious Leaders

"Dr. Migliore's Pastor's Workshop was great. The information was all a new concept to me, but I can see the extreme wealth in following through with it."

"I don't want to sound overly dramatic, but I literally fell on my knees and praised God for the wisdom that filled my mind and spirit because of your presentation."

"I now have a plan of action and a way to channel my faith."

"Praise God for these wonderful Pastor's Workshops. I look forward eagerly to the next session."

"Thank you for the opportunity to see the Pastor's Workshop. It was excellent."

"I would like to say how much I enjoyed the pastor's workshop. I learned a tremendous amount."

"The pastor's workshop was very helpful and informational. I am looking forward to the next session."

"I am finding these Pastor's seminars exceptional. I will be able to use these MBO principles very effectively."

"Thank you very much. I really appreciated the Pastor's Workshop. We expect to incorporate the MBO approach."

"We appreciated the information shared during the seminar and believe that it is an answer to many of our prayers."

"Thank you again for another quality performance."

"I really want to thank you because this has been so helpful."

"I feel this is where the majority of Charismatic ministries have missed it. They have been too spiritual to spend any time planning."

"Thank you for having Dr. Migliore help us out here in the field. I look forward to the next workshop."

"May we express how much we enjoyed your seminar, and we are most enthusiastic about implementing the ideas and information presented to us."

"May I take this opportunity to express my personal appreciation for the excellent training being made available to the church body. We will succeed when we are taught to operate in excellent ways."

". . . really enjoyed participating in these workshops and have found them to be a great tool in the ministry."

"With Dr. Migliore's help and this planning process, we know we can continue to become the kind of church God wants us to be."

Dr. James Buskirk
The First United Methodist Church
Tulsa, Oklahoma

"Without adequate long-range plans, we will miss many opportunities. However, through your assistance we will capitalize on the potential God has given us."

> Billy Joe Daugherty
> Victory Christian Center
> Tulsa, Oklahoma

"Our management staff was relatively unfamiliar with the concepts of 'Management By Objectives,' but Dr. Migliore was able to quickly teach the elements involved in the MBO approach. He gained the confidence of our top management team and in a relatively short period of time helped us in developing long-range objectives for the organization."

> Brian Erickson
> Executive Director
> *Back to the Bible Broadcast*
> Lincoln, Nebraska

"My 30-year career as a YMCA profesional has allowed me to work with, participate in, and give leadership to long-range planning projects in other associations throughout the country. I can quickly and openly attest that the high quality work performed by Dean Migliore in our recent Tulsa YMCA project exceeds all other experiences."

> Ray A. Pfeiffer
> The Young Men's Christian Association
>   of Greater Tulsa
> Tulsa, Oklahoma

"Because of the positive effect it is having on our entire church, we consider our decision to develop a five-year plan the most important goal of 1986."

> Dale A. Brooks
> Calvary Temple
> International Christian Center
> Temple Terrace, Florida

"Migliore played a crucial role in the development of an administrative plan for the growing ministries of the Christian Legal Society . . . ."

> Lynn Robert Buzzard
> (Formerly with Christian Legal Society)
> Oak Park, Illinois

"All of my top executives that have been privileged down through the years to attend the meetings that you have chaired here have been greatly enriched. Their jobs have become more meaningful as a result of being filled with great management purposes and clear objective."

> Morris Cerullo
> President, World Evangelism
> San Diego, California

"We are just beginning the process under the guidance of Dr. Migliore and are already excited and expectant of great worthwhile results."

> Ernest J. Lewis, Pastor
> First Presbyterian Church
> Tulsa, Oklahoma

Appendix B

Strategic Planning Sequence

Church management develops purpose through organization strategy

Board of Directors, Elders or Executive Committee approves plan	First level of organization; music, youth, etc.	Budget for next operating year developed	All plans, budgets at every level refined for coming year to execute plan	Organization goes to work. Objectives set to lowest levels	Group review progress toward achievement of objectives
July	August	September October	November December January	February March	April May

Individual review of progress toward achievement of objectives	Group review of progress toward achievement of objectives		Final year end review of results. Salary recommendation based on performance	Bonus approved based on performance
June	July	August	September October	November December January	February March

157

Appendix C

ACTION PLAN

OBJECTIVE:

STRATEGIES:

    A.

    B.

    C.

    D.

    E.

ACTION PLAN	PERSON RESPONSIBLE	START DATE	DATE COMPLETED

Appendix D

I. Purpose

   A. What is "Reason for Being"?

II. Environmental Analysis

   A. Pulse

   B. Now or Past

   C. Surveys

   D. Studies or Future done now

III. S & W

   A. Human

   B. Facilities

   C. Resources

   D. Patents

IV. Assumptions

   A. You have no control over

   B. Extend Environmental Analysis

V. Objectives and Goals

   A. Specific, time frame, measurable in key result areas. Not all rules for objectives. Should be for a minimum of five years.

VI.   Strategy
     A. Thinking stage
     B. Where commit resources
     C. Timing

VII. L.R.P.
     A. Doing something in future
     B. How?
     C. Build, Hire, Fire
     D. Keep out results
     E. Develop proforma income/balance sheets

VIII. S.R.P.
     A. What do this year, this quarter
     B. Keep out results
     C. First year of five-year plan

Appendix E

The following is a quick review of what has been covered. Examples of the situation I found at Continental Can Company in 1967-68 and a church plan are given.

1967-68

	Continental Can	Church
Purpose	Survival and profit in the packaging business	Serve God Evangelize Heal Sick
Environmental	Pork prices, trends in new packages	Unemployment high in our country
Strengths	Knowledgeable managers; poor organization	Old church building in need of repair, no debts
Objectives	Cut M.E. efficiency loss of — 17% by April 1968 to break even	Increase attendance at all services by 10% next year
Strategy	Go after the fruit packers, government business	Use more participation by people in service

Long-Range Plan	Relocate department in stages over next five years	Build a new church
Short-Range Plan	Follow the MBO plan for the year and the budget	Ask for bids on church building
Appraisal and Recycling	Ran ten weeks straight in black April 15, 1968	Last year attendance down by 6%

Appendix F

Case Studies:
Victory Christian Center/
Calvary Temple/Back to the Bible

Victory Christian Center of Tulsa, Oklahoma, under the leadership of Billy Joe Daugherty, and Calvary Temple of Tampa, Florida, under the leadership of Dale Brooks, are two good recent examples of how ministries can use the concepts of strategic planning and management to get organized and meet the potential God has given them. The format they followed can be used by any church or ministry as a guide to getting started. It is interesting to note a number of things that both ministries have in common. Some of the things I have noted that they have in common include: growing ministries over the past five years, in an urban setting, led by warm, communicative, people-oriented pastors, and a sense of the Holy Spirit in their services.

In both cases, Pastors Daugherty and Brooks came to me with the request to help them develop a planning and management system in their ministries. It is important for the long-term success of any planning effort to have the enthusiasm and backing of the senior pastor. Both have confirmed in conversations with me that they realize one of the keys to reach the potential in the ministry was that the planning and management system had to grow and handle the ever-changing needs and grow right along with the size of the ministry itself.

In all types of organizations it has been noted that many founders continued to try to plan, organize, manage, and communicate the same way they did when they started. As staffs get bigger and the mission becomes more complex, with more and more departments, volunteers, and people involved, it is imperative that the management system become more sophisticated to handle the changing needs.

Credit is due both pastors for being able to see and understand this principle early in their ministries. In most churches and ministries, change is initiated only after turmoil, sometimes spanning years, before any changes are made in the planning and management system. Both of these pastors can see this problem before they reach it and are now getting their organizations ready with a strong foundation for the future. Both men used my books and materials as learning guides. Both set up committees and got people involved, following the format prescribed in the books. There were times with both groups when we all wondered if we were ever going to get a plan together. I confidently knew that progress was being made, even with the countless number of manhours put into the planning process. Sometimes I think it is better to take a long time to get the plan together because that is one way for everyone to better understand it. And because both ministry situations were complex, input was needed from all sources to finally get the strategic direction in place. The Lord was not left out of the planning process. I observed plenty of prayer going into confirming all steps of the planning process.

Once the plans started taking place, one could just sense the excitement of staff members and all people involved in the management of the ministries. The total potential is still there for both ministries, and it will be interesting to see where they are ten and twenty years from now. I firmly believe that the time taken to build this foundation is going to put them in a position to be of great service to the Lord and to mankind.

I also believe a foundation has been built to meet the needs of the people in both ministries. The old adage that "those who execute the plan need to be in on the plan" was met in every step of the planning cycle. No one was left out. Everyone was involved. One could feel a great sense of participation, enthusiasm, and excitement, both in the meetings and wherever one ran into people associated with both ministries. It has been my observation in many ministries throughout the world that the needs of the employees are often forgotten, and great anxiety, dissatisfaction, and frustration are rampant. If anything, ministries should be the best places in America to work. Sadly, in many cases, they are the worst. It does not make sense for IBM, Xerox, Sears, and other organizations to have the edge on being great places to work. If things continue as they are, I predict that Victory Christian Center and Calvary Temple will continue to be great places to work. I have noticed that the *Back to the Bible Broadcast* in Lincoln, Nebraska, had very little turnover in the ten years that I have been working with them. *Back to the Bible Broadcast* is a great place to work. It consistently scores high on my attitude survey ratings, and there's a great love and concern for people there. I believe it should be this way in all ministries. The *Broadcast* is one of the best managed groups with which I have had the opportunity to work.

It is interesting to note some of the benefits that both Victory and Calvary attained from implementing this planning and management system. Both used this system as a tool and instrument to measure progress within their departments. Each department had to complete a plan for its area, which in turn would fit into the overall plan for the ministry. It was during this stage of the planning process that Calvary Temple realized the necessity to develop a clearly defined chain of command within their organizational structure. The results were far reaching. Each department began to see how it was a vital part of the ministry, thus promoting a "team concept" within the organization. For example, it was exciting to observe how the maintenance department operates at Calvary. Those involved believe that they are called by God into their department, not as a job, but as a ministry, and without them the overall ministry at Calvary Temple would not be complete.

In developing a plan for the overall ministry at Calvary Temple, a vision for the church evolved with specific goals to achieve that vision. This gave the ministry a sense of direction not only of where it is going, but also a plan of how to get there. Several years ago Pastor Brooks had a vision for a congregation of 5,000 members. The elders and those involved in the planning process began to see how this could be achieved by 1991 through proper planning and goal setting. At one point in the process there were more than one hundred persons out of the congregation involved in planning who were basically uninvolved before I began working with them. The people began to rally around the pastor's dream and support his vision. Growth does not take place without a vision, but many do not realize that the vision needs to center on where God has placed them — in their Jerusalem.

Pastor Brooks realizes this principle and is using planning to reach the people of the Tampa Bay area for Christ. It is interesting to note that this goal evolved through much prayer and waiting on the Holy Spirit for direction. Once that direction was given, the people were able to "run with the vision," as stated in Habakkuk 2:2. I see no reason to believe that they will not reach this goal and then strive for even higher goals as God directs.

At Victory Christian Center planning has also helped to provide a tool that is being used to more effectively manage. Victory is a church that has witnessed explosive growth over the past few years — since their inception seven years ago they average more than 7,000 people in attendance during Sunday-morning service. As the church has grown, so has the organization. In any business or ministry that expands as quickly as this, there is the opportunity to let the "tail wag the dog." Victory realized that their purpose, or reason for being, was to meet the needs of the people that God entrusted to them. As a result the leadership developed a five-fold ministry that includes praise and worship, prayer, preaching and teaching, fellowship, and evangelism. Before a management decision is made at Victory, the ministerial staff prays about the matter to see if it is in agreement with their purpose. God has called them to do a specific work. Their desire is to strive towards fulfilling that calling which God has given them. In doing this a sense of direction and unity to the staff and congregation at Victory has been developed. They know what their calling is, and all pull together as a team to reach out towards that calling.

One of the keys to the success of any ministry is the ability of its leader to have visions and dreams, and then communicate these visions and dreams to the people. Once again, we need to remember what Proverbs 29:18 says: **Where there is no vision, the people perish.**

One of the biggest benefits of the planning and management system at Victory is that it has united the congregation around a vision that includes specific and measurable goals for the next five years. Victory developed a plan and then put it into writing. This helped unite the body at Victory around one purpose, striving towards the same goals. As each department developed plans, a sense of excitement was created. Everyone was working towards the same goals. The nursery department could make projections based upon the five-year goals of the church. Likewise, the budget system was developed for the next five years, incorporating the goals and projections that were developed by the church and each of its departments. As a final step, individuals developed personal plans for their lives, which enabled them to achieve personal as well as vocational growth.

Appendix G

Responses From People Attending a Recent Strategic Planning Seminar

WHAT WILL THIS SEMINAR DO FOR
THE COMPANY?

1. "Gives top management the chance to help develop the path of travel during the next five years."

2. "Gives us a soap box to voice our true feelings."

3. "Gives us a chance to formulate and consolidate ideas and to mature."

4. "Gives us a format to follow."

5. "Helps organize and clarify communication from top down."

6. "Involves all employees in a way that can be managed."

7. "Gives us faith internally in helping our financial status."

8. "We will now have a better defined objective to market."

9. "Develop a real business atmosphere and teamwork in an already healthy management team."

10. "Help those of us who are leaders to field problems before they become just that in a way that effects the overall plan in a positive way

11. "It places into effect controls on past temptations to yield to whims and impetuousness."

12. "Provides basis for decision making."

13. "Provides measurable goals and the attendant reward that comes with accomplishment."

14. "Creates a forum for all levels of management to have a steering influence on company direction."

15. "Helps us deal with contingent circumstances and less with panic."

16. "Helps all employees to define reason to rally."

17. "Employees will be more ready to fully participate and make commitments."

18. "Enables us to work as a team in becoming financially successful."

19. "Helps everyone realize reaching our goals in going to take hard work and teamwork, but will be worth the effort."

20. "Gives team direction, makes for more labor and cost-effective measures, and sets the stage for more productivity."

YOU CAN HAVE THE SAME RESULTS

WHAT WILL THIS SEMINAR DO FOR ME AS AN INDIVIDUAL?

1. "Help me develop methods in management decision making."

2. "Help me plan objectives."

3. "Help me produce finished plans for management responsibilities."

4. "Enable me to set a definite direction and go for it."

5. "Let me know that I am an important part of the team and that the team feels the same way."

6. "Gives me the tools, support, and encouragement to contribute to and reach team goals."

7. "Gives me a sense that communication is improving."

8. "Will make me more efficient, more goal oriented."

9. "This strategic planning can be used in full or in part in all of life's challenges and opportunities."

10. "De-personalizes difficult management decisions."

11. "Helps me develop measurable targets so that subordinates can be more easily evaluated."

12. "This plan will steer me away from frustration and discouragement."

13. "The ability to use one's gifts and strengths one's weaker points is of greater importance."

14. "Get me organized in a way that will create results."

15. "Give me more job satisfaction, make me more active part of the whole."

16. "Make me more efficient and help my growth."

17. "Force me to become the most effective manager possible."

18. "A very powerful and directional place for a person to start."

19. "With this plan, my potential can be tremendous."

20. "Boosts my morale and gives me a clearer, overall picture to achieve my desired goals."

YOU CAN HAVE THE SAME RESULTS

Appendix H

Your Church Has a Fantastic Future
by
Robert H. Schuller
(Comments by R. Henry Migliore)

I. Seven Principles of Success."
    The seven principles of success are:
    1. Accessibility — church should be easy to find
    2. Surplus parking — have more than enough parking
    3. Inventory — means have enough programs to meet needs
    4. Service — recruit, train, and motivate lay people
    5. Visibility — in the public eye
    6. Possibility thinking — asking right questions, thinking stategically
    7. Good cash flow — managing your money and others.

    The organizations in this article are analyzed as to their use of each of these principles.

    1. Victory Christian Center, Tulsa, Oklahoma:
        They have strategically placed themselves on South Lewis Avenue with access to four lanes and expressway.
    2. Mt. Zion, Greenville, South Carolina:
        As they planned to meet their objective of

moving into a new sanctuary in Spring of 1988 they provided parking for 4,200.

3. First United Methodist, Tulsa, Oklahoma: They have four Sunday services, twenty-three outside ministries and meet almost every conceivable need of their members.

4. Calvary Temple, Tampa, Florida: Their congregation of lay people are working in every part of the ministry.

5. Mother Tucker, Tulsa, Oklahoma: She has a way of keeping her ministry in front of the people and in the news.

6. *Back to the Bible Broadcast*, Lincoln, Nebraska: They have done an excellent job of planning, growing, and controlling their funds.

Every one of the churches listed here are thinking big, reaching out, and dreaming. The fact that they have asked me to help tells me they want to control their own destiny.

II. Eleven Attitudes that Hinder Growth:

1. Church growth just happens

2. Detachment from the world

3. Boredom

4. Negative emotions

5. Denominational success

6. Fear of debt

7. Lack of conviction

8. Distracted from primacy mission

9. The controversial pulpit

10. Short-sighted leadership

11. Impossibility thinking

None of the churches and ministries with whom I am working today suffer to a great degree with these problems. I have noticed three that looked at my concepts, took a brief whirl with it, and have many of the problems listed above. All three have lost ground over the past few years.

Appendix I

MBO Performance Appraisal Form
for Minister of Music

	Excellent 5	Above Average 4	Average 3	Below Average 2	Poor 1	Discussion Notes
1. Operate within budget of $12,000	5					
2. Average 95/choir attendance	5					
3. Four special programs a year		4				
4. Attend one music workshop	5					
5. Set up children's choir			3			
	18	4	3			22 = Total

	Excellent 5	Above Average 4	Average 3	Below Average 2	Poor 1	Discussion Notes
1. Use of LRP/MBO	5					
2. Developing people	5					
3. Contribution to morale	5					
4. Communication			3			
5. Creativity	5					
6. Emotional stability	5					
7. Job knowledge		4				
8. What kind of leader	5					
9. Problem solver			3			
10. Public image	5					
	35	4	6			

Average of objectives = 22   5 = 4.4
Average of other items = 45   10 = 4.5
Weighted avergage = (4.4 x 75) + (4.5 x 25) = 4.425

Acknowledgements

I wish to thank the following people for their contribution to the study and this article; Elaine Drain and Marcella Rogers for original typing from ORU's Word Processing Center and Lorri Metz of Facet Enterprises, Inc. who made all the revisions; thanks to Mike Kelly for his fine work on graphics and visuals; Connie Blackwell, James A Ferrier, and the late Lynn Nichols for their outstanding editing skills; Ruth Jeffries who helped coordinate correspondence with all pastors; the professional staff at Word of Faith Outreach Center, under the direction of Al Brice who made it all possible; Dr. Larry Lacour's graduate theology class who gave constructive ideas; Elizabeth Lee and Jeff Horvath for their valuable help with the studies and their analysis; and the following pastors for their ideas and suggestions:

Rev. Ron Bakken, Word and Faith Fellowship, Moorehead, MN

Pastors James and Genelle Bloom, Faith Chapel, Winoma, KS

Rev. Melvin Brand, Faith Covenant Fellowship, Estes Park, CO

Rev. D. L. Van Brunt, Christian Life Center, Albuquerque, NM

Rev. Bill Burgess, England Word of Faith, England, AR

Dr. James Buskirk, First United Methodist Church, Tulsa, OK

Pastors Rich and Sheri Carbone, Cornerstone Life Church, Tacoma, WA

Mark Cerver, World Vision, Monrovia, CA

Pastors Dino and Marilyn Costas, New Jerusalem Church, Potomac, MD

Pastors John and Linda Cummings, Word of Life Fellowship, Wasilla, AK

Rev. E. Patrick Fadden, Crossroad Word Faith Center, Surry, BC

Rev. Burket Farrell, Christian Life Center, Morrisville, VT

Rev. Gregory Fletcher, Overcoming-Faith Chapel, Middletown, Ohio

Rev. Joe Frye, Greater Faith Christian Center, Ann Arbor, MI

Rev. Jerry Hatlevig, Assembly of God Church, Sauk Centre, MN

Rev. Don Hudson, Grace Fellowship Church, Oneonta, AL

Timothy King, Emmanuel Fellowship, Plainfield, CN

Rev. Dale A. Brooks, Calvary Temple International Christian Center, Temple Terrace, FL

Rev. Lynn Robert Buzzard, Christian Legal Society, Oak Park, IL

Rev. Morris Cerullo, President, World Evangelism, San Diego, CA

Rev. Billy Joe Daugherty, Victory Christian Center, Tulsa, OK

Rev. Brian Erickson, Executive Director, Back-to-the Bible Broadcast, Lincoln, NE

Rev. Peter Knapp, Faith Fellowship, West Mystic, CT

Rev. Jeff Korsen, North Christian Fellowship, North Glen, CO

Rev. Ray Larson, Bethel Church, Redding, CA

Rev. David Mallonee, Living Word Center, Springfield, MO

Rev. Dennis L. Matula, Jubilee Christian Faith Center, Hastings, MN

Rev. Reagan Miller, Westbank Revival Center, Gretna, LA

Rev. Alberto Olive, Word of Faith and Teaching Center, Atlanta, GA

Rev. Ray Pfeiffer, The Young Men's Christian Association of Greater Tulsa, Tulsa, OK

Rev. Scott Stecher, New Creation Fellowship Church, Grand Junction, CO

Rev. Ron Tannariello, Living Faith Ministries, Merrimack, NH

Rev. Lloyd Thomforde, Sowers of the Word Fellowship, Wanamingo, MN

Rev. David Thomas, Metro Church, Edmond, OK

Rev. Daniel Turos, Redemption Center Word Fellowship, Florissant, MO

Rev. W. T. Wozencraft, Word of Faith Christian Center, Weatherford, TX

Rev. Randy Wren, Faith Fellowship, Santa Fe, NM

Glenn Edwards, Calgary, Canada

Pastor Warren Wiersbe, Back to the Bible, Lincoln, NE

Rev. Ernest Lewis, First Presbyterian Church, Tulsa, OK

Rev. Brad Lewis, Mt. Zion, Greenville, SC

Annotated Bibliography

Holy Bible, Proverbs 15:22, "Without counsel purposes are disappointed; but in the multitude of counselors they are established."

Holy Bible, Proverbs 19:20, "Hear counsel, and receive instruction, that thou mayest be wise in the latter end."

Holy Bible, Proverbs 20:18a, "Every purpose is established by counsel."

Holy Bible, Proverbs 21:30, "There is no wisdom nor understanding nor counsel against the Lord."

Holy Bible, Proverbs 24:3,4, "Through wisdom is an house builded; and by understanding it is established: And by knowledge shall the chambers be filled with all precious and pleasant riches."

Holy Bible, Proverbs 29:18, "Where there is no vision, the people perish: but he that keepeth the law, happy is he."

Holy Bible, Joel 2:28, "And it shall come to pass afterward, that I will pour out my spirit upon all flesh; and your sons and your daughters shall prophesy, your old men shall dream dreams, your young men shall see visions."

Holy Bible, Luke 13:32, "Go ye, and tell that fox, Behold, I cast out devils and I do cures to

day and to morrow and the third day I
shall be perfected."

Holy Bible, Acts 2:17, ". . . And your young men shall
see visions, and your old men shall dream
dreams."

Holy Bible, Philippians 3:14, "I press toward the mark
for the prize of the high calling of God in
Christ Jesus."

Matt. 16:17-19; Matt. 18:18-20; Matt. 28:18-20; Mark
16:16; Luke 18:19-21; John 2:21; John 20:22; Acts 1:8; Acts
2:38-41; Acts 8:1; 1 Cor. 1:2; 1 Cor. 3:16,17; 1 Cor. 12:4,6,
12-14, 28; Eph. 1:7; Eph. 4:3-6; Col. 1:2,18; Heb. 8:12;
1 Pet. 2:9,10; Rev. 11:2,9.

Matt. 18:15-17; Mark 11:25,26; Luke 24:46-48; 1 Cor.
5:6; 2 Cor. 5:20,21; Eph. 4:1-3; Eph. 5:22-24; 1 Thess.
2:12; 1 Thess. 5:13; 2 Tim. 1:7; Titus 3:1; Philem. 1:17,18;
Heb. 10:25; 1 Pet. 5:5,6? 1 John 2:3,5; 1 John 4:7-12, 16.

Church and Community Survey Workbook, 1970. (Nashville,
Convention Press):
A "must" for any group that wants to gather
information.

Leading Your Church in Long-Range Planning, 1975.
(Nashville: Convention Press).
This is a very well-thought-out book put out
by the Southern Baptist Convention. It is well
written, has good guidelines, and practical
examples. It agrees in many ways with the
theory and practice behind my own work.

Additional copies
Available from
your local bookstore,
or from:

P. O. Box 35035
Tulsa, Oklahoma 74153

My Books

An MBO Approach to Long-Range Planning
> Focus is on expanding MBO into a long-range planning system

Common Sense Management
> Taking all I have learned and stating the principles in plain terms

Develop A Strategic Plan for Your Life
> All the planning concepts I have used in my work adapted to help people develop a plan for their lives

MBO: Blue Collar To Top Executive
> Focus is on using MBO at lower levels

Strategic Long-Range Planning
> An update of previous books, materials, studies, newspaper columns.

Tales of Uncle Henry
> Adventures I have had in the outdoors over past 20 years

To contact Dr. Migliore,
write:

R. Henry Migliore
P. O. Box 957
Jenks, Oklahoma 74037

*Please include your prayer requests
and comments when you write.*

About the Author

R. Henry Migliore of Jenks, Oklahoma, is Facet Enterprises Professor of Strategic Planning and Management, Northeastern State University/University Center at Tulsa. Dr. Migliore teaches at the graduate and undergraduate levels. He served as professor of management and as dean of the ORU School of Business from 1975 until 1987.

He is a former manager of the press manufacturing operations of Continental Can Company's Stockyard Plant. Prior to that, he was responsible for the industrial engineering function at Continental's Indiana plant. In this capacity, Dr. Migliore was responsible for coordinating the long-range planning process. In addition, he has had various consulting experiences with Fred Rudge & Associates in New York and has served large and small businesses, associations and nonprofit organizations in various capacities.

He has made presentations to a wide variety of clubs, groups, and professional associations.

Dr. Migliore has been selected to be on the faculty for the International Conferences on Management by Objectives and the Strategic Planning Institute Seminar Series. He is also a frequent contributor to the Academy of Management, including the presentation of a paper at the 50th anniversary national conference.

He is on the Board of Directors of T. D. Williamson, Inc., the American Red Cross/Tulsa Chapter, and was previously on the board of the International MBO

Institute, and Brush Creek Ranch. He also is chairman of a scholarship fund for Eastern State College. In 1984, he was elected into the Eastern State College Athletic Hall of Fame. Dr. Migliore has been a guest lecturer on a number of college campuses. He serves on four Chamber/Civic Committees, and is on the Administrative Board at The First United Methodist Church, Tulsa, and the Board of American Red Cross/Tulsa Chapter.

To date previous articles on management and business subjects have appeared in *AII E Journal*, *Construction News*, *Management World*, *Management of Personnel Quarterly*, *Journal of Long-Range Planning*, *Dental Economics*, *Health Care Management Review*, *MBO Journal*, *Business and Society Review*, *Parks and Recreation Journal*, *The Journal of Business Strategy*, *Daily Blessing*, *Ozark Mountaineer*, *On Line*, *Real Estate Today*, and the *Planning Review*.

His books, *MBO: Blue Collar to Top Executive*, *An MBO Approach to Long-Range Planning*, *A Strategic Plan for Your Life*, *and* Strategic Long-Range Planning, describe personal theories and experiences. He contributed to the books, *Readings in Interpersonal and Organizational Communication* and *International Handbook on MBO*.

The manuscript, *Production/Operations Management: A Productivity Approach* is being co-authored and will be published in 1988. *Common Sense Management, The Use of Strategic Planning in Churches and Ministries*, and *Tales of Uncle Henry* are in the manuscript stage and also will be published in 1988.

Dr. Migliore produced "Personal Financial Success," an Oral Roberts Ministry video training kit offered on nationwide television, and video/audio tapes to go with his books.

In November 1985, the daily "Managing for Success" cable television program was inaugurated and was on the air until March 1986 on Tulsa Cable. The series began again on Tulsa Cable in September 1986.

In addition, Dr. Migliore is a guest columnist with *The Tulsa Tribune* and contributes a sports feature to the *Jenks Journal*.

Dr. Migliore holds degrees from Eastern Oklahoma State, Oklahoma State University, and St. Louis University, and completed his doctorate at the University of Arkansas. He belongs to the Academy of Management, Planning Executives Institute, and is a senior member of the American Institute of Industrial Engineers.